INTO THE
HEART OF THE INFINITE

Into the Heart of the Infinite

A Spiritual Memoir of an
Extraordinary Mystical Journey

Maetreyii Ma Nolan, PhD

Published by
Ananda Guru Kula Publications
Santa Rosa, California

© 2024 Maetreyii Ma, M. E. Nolan, Ph.D.
All Rights Reserved

Editing and Compilation by
Rosina Tinari Wilson
Proof Reading by Kathleen McTeigue

Cover Art by Peter Weltevrede
Design and Layout by Zizi Subiyarta (PGTN Design)

Dedicated to
My Baba

Shrii Shrii Anandamurti

$\mathcal{N}$ot everyone is fortunate enough to meet his or her *guru* in physical form. I feel blessed as this opportunity has been a part of my life. My guru, Shrii Shrii Anandamurti, walked this earth from 1921 until 1990. He lived in northern India, Bihar, and Bengal, where he taught the ancient traditions of classical North Indian *Tantra* and *Ashtanga Yoga*.

As you will soon read, I had an opportunity to spend almost a year in India receiving his *darshan*, seeing him, hearing his talks, and having profound experiences. Baba was purported to speak in two hundred languages and could talk to all those who came to see him in their native tongues. It is said that on several occasions, he was seen visiting people in one location while he was giving a talk at another nearly five hundred miles away. I personally observed many miracles occurring around him – people going into states of divine bliss simply from his glance or touch, healings, and people's lives changed.

Waves of divine bliss accompanied him when he entered a room, and he clearly knew everything about those present, including your deepest core feelings. He was an ocean of love, a true, realized Master. When people looked into his eyes, they saw the universe.

It was said that as a small boy of about five years, while walking alone in the jungle, he encountered a pillar of whitelight. When he asked who it was, the pillar told him it was Shrii Shrii Anandamurti. When it enfolded him in the light, the boy became the Master.

The experiences of Baba communicated in the following pages are an expression of the immutable love of the Divine, both as a physical guru and as an inner guide. Many, many other experiences of this love can be told by others. Such love is not given to one person but to all. The Divine expresses infinite love and grace in many ways, and I am sure will continue to express it to all who turn to him/her with sincerity and conviction.

Table of Contents

Introduction

*I*n the quiet corners of our lives, amid the ceaseless hum of the everyday, many of us have felt it—a whisper, a pull, an ineffable sense of something more. It's a beckoning towards the Infinite, the Divine, an invitation to step beyond the known and plunge into the mystic depths of existence. This memoir is the story of how that call has unfolded in my life.

My journey, which I lay bare in these pages, is deeply personal. It is a journey of love that I write about. The journey of my heart and soul. Marked by Divine visitations from childhood through profound psychedelic revelations, the embrace of yogic disciplines, and a spiritual pilgrimage to India—a land that seemed to hold the keys to the sacred—it leads to a calling and revelations that could not be ignored.

This story brings the mystical quest into view. Yet, this is not just my story. It is a story resonant with every soul that yearns, that questions, that loves passionately. *Into the Heart of the Infinite* is more than a tale of spiritual discovery; it is an odyssey of the soul's calling, a testament to the transformative power of love, surrender, and the grace of the Eternal One.

As you traverse this narrative, you may see reflections of your own doubts, your own epiphanies, and your own indomitable spirit. My hope is that as I share my communion with the Divine—both as an inner, guiding presence and in the physical form of a guru in India—you will be inspired to listen to your own heart's calling and embark on the greatest adventure of all: the journey to truly know your deepest Self.

In these pages, you will find not just my story—but an echo of the universal quest for meaning, connection, and a deeper understanding of the vast, beautiful enigma that is our existence. Welcome to a pilgrimage of the heart, a journey Into the Heart of the Infinite.

This introduction sets the stage for a profound exploration of spirituality and personal transformation, inviting you to explore your own inner journey as you relate to the passages shared in this memoir.

With loving thoughts, Maetreyii Ma

www.maetreyiima.org   https://linktr.ee/maetreyiima

Author's Note

*A*ll poetry included in these pages are the original writings of Maetreyii Ma unless otherwise specified. The poems are included because some deep feelings are difficult to communicate and are best expressed in the poetic language of the heart. The poems have been written over the years when a mood of divine love and ecstatic being has wanted to weave an expression of the communion of the soul into form.

The Divine is neither male nor female, but beyond such distinctions, yet the pronoun "he" is often used in this text to refer to the Divine. This is both because there is no neutral pronoun in the English language and due to the fact that the form in which the Divine manifests most frequently for me has a male ambiance, though, in truth, the Infinite has no gender, or perhaps all genders.

A few Sanskrit terms important to yogic philosophy and practice, or to the story being told, are used, as their meaning is more precise in Sanskrit. They are usually defined immediately after the word. However, for the convenience of readers wanting more extensive definitions or who are not familiar with these terms, they are also defined in a glossary. Additional non-English terms relevant to the text are also included in the glossary.

www.maetreyiima.org   https://linktr.ee/maetreyiima

Into the Heart of the Infinite
Prologue

*I*n my age of wisdom, I pause to reflect upon my journey of spirit, and the ups and downs of life that have brought me to the depths of my soul. I have come to know that there is only one eternal, immortal flow of being. The illusion of a separate self weaves a dream we call our lives. But beneath this outer shell lies a vast realm of love, divine essence, and aware consciousness. This is the Self of ourselves, the interior castle, the realm of light and blessedness. I have come to realize that this is the true treasure of human life. From this interior realm, a flow of knowledge and love—of teachings far beyond anything my mind can conceive—have arisen to guide my life and the lives of others.

It was not always like this. I did not always feel this grace, this omniscient love. By a power far beyond me, I have been guided step by step, experience by experience, to the numinous. This is the story of how this realization and grace unfolded. It is perhaps not so much my story as the story of how the Infinite can manifest in our world and transform our lives.

Chapter I
The Beginning

I was young, perhaps nine or ten, when a sense of an unknown destiny first wove itself through the threads of my mind. It was a prelude to a future I could not have imagined.

I am playing by myself in my upstairs room. As I look around, I see a low-angled ceiling on one side and brown flowered wallpaper throughout. A girlish vanity stands against the far wall, and a print of a painting with a man on a mountain path hangs above my bed. Lying across my bed, I stare for hours at this painting. All kinds of stories come alive in my imagination.

Musing in my room, a stirring begins within me. I begin to wonder about myself. I start to sense something at the edge of my awareness, a feeling of a foregone destiny, something I know I am to do in my life, though I have no idea what it is.

I see a triangular shape form in my mind's eye and realize that this triangle represents my journey in life. I see myself at the bottom of the triangle, ranging from side to side in the broadest part. Then I see, as my life goes on, that I will move up the pyramid to the apex, and, reaching the peak, the topmost point, I will understand this destiny.

From this moment of childhood, musing onward, I knew there was a reason, a purpose, for my being. Something I would discover as life went on. Something that gave meaning to my life. Though I did not understand it, I knew it was something I had somehow once agreed to do.

A Child's Journey

I was about two when we moved out of Chicago into an outlying suburb. My parents, wanting to leave the city, bought a mini farm of about five acres, which turned out to be my haven of connection to the natural world. We had several hundred chickens, a few pigs, a dozen or so geese, a dog named Pal, several cats, my pet duck Jimmy, and wild raccoons.

There was a river down in the woods, and a small stream ran off it through the property with a wooden bridge we had to cross to get to the barn and chicken yard. Wild blackberries and raspberries grew along the creek, and wild strawberries in the front, near the long drive that meandered to the lilac hedge between us and the gravel road. There were fruit trees in the front yard, primarily apples; lightning bugs, and butterflies; and my mother's garden out back.

At that time, I was a gentle, free-roaming child with freckles and long, wavy, golden-red hair that always managed to escape its confines, despite my mother's best efforts to keep it in its braids. I would run wild in nature, eating berries and playing with Jimmy, Pal, or my cats. In the mornings, I would say hi to the pigs, look in on the geese, and watch the baby ducklings swimming in the stream. My mom and I would work in the garden, filling bushel baskets with fresh vegetables, shelling peas, and feeding chickens. And I would catch butterflies and lightning bugs in the evenings while my parents watched from the porch.

Our house back then was simple, without running water. We had an outhouse, a pump for water, and a big potbelly stove in the living room. I used to sit at night and watch the flames. I remember it was cold in the bedrooms, so my mom heated bricks by the fire for the beds.

There was a small shed on our little farm where my dad stored corn he harvested. It had a trapdoor leading to the cellar where my mom stacked her canning on shelves every year, from floor to ceiling. My two older brothers, Bob and Harry, and my Irish grandma Margaret lived in our humble house with my mom, dad, and me. Generally, times were sweet then.

The Little Girl Who Loved Nature

A Taste of Spiritualism

I don't remember much of my journey of spirit from that time, besides being melded into my animals and woods and being a bit of a wild spirit. But there was one day in those earlier years when something unusual did happen. It was one of my earliest memories. My parents took me to see an extraordinary man at our neighbors' house.

They put on their go-to-church clothes and dressed me in a nice outfit. We got in the car and drove around the block to see our neighbors. Then my mom took my hand, and we walked to the door where our neighbors met us. My dad picked me up and brought me in, putting me down on the living room floor, where I watched as they approached a mysterious-looking man. I looked up from my small vantage point and could feel something different about him. He was unusual looking as well, with very white, light hair and pale skin. I think my parents said he was an albino. He was dressed in white also.

My parents, this man, and our neighbors gathered around a big table in the room, maybe seven feet from where I sat on the floor. Then they put their hands flat on this big old dining room table. It was the heavy kind, with large acorn legs. They laid their hands on the tabletop, and I heard a creaking sound. With wide eyes and an open mouth, I looked up at the big legs and table bottom as it began to shake and lift off the floor, six to eight inches! Much to my awe, it just stayed there, suspended in the air for what seemed a long time. I was bewildered.

They all had their hands on the top of the table. No one was holding it up! Finally, the table again began to shake and creak a bit. Then it settled to the floor. I wondered as I watched, *"What just happened? Who is this strange man?"*

After that, the man got up and talked to each person, perhaps about their futures. After a time, my parents called me over to introduce me to him. I was very reluctant, but I got up and shuffled over, head down, trying to be invisible. When I got to my mom, awed and shy, I clung to her skirt, hiding in the folds. I knew this man was different from other people. I could feel it. I think he was telling my parents something about me as I stood there, but I couldn't hear.

I must have been only three or four at the time. Yet this experience stuck with me. As an adult, I learned it was likely an example of Spiritualism, which was popular then. In retrospect, it helped me realize that the impossible can be possible. At the time, I just accepted what happened. It was part of my life on the farm, as were my grandma and my mom's sisters.

The Second Sight

I was always told that the "Second Sight" ran with the women in our family. From what my mom and aunts said, it was part of our Irish heritage, this ability to know the future and distant events. My mom came from a large Irish Catholic family with twelve brothers and sisters in which red or auburn hair, along with strong mystical and psychic inclinations, abounded.

They said my grandma had the sight, as did my mom and her sisters. My grandma was a refined Irish lady. I remember Gran singing Irish ditties with me, crocheting, speaking with a brogue, and teatime with her in the afternoons. In those years when my grandma was with us, we saw my mom's family often. My aunts visited several times a week. Picnics and other family events were common.

Grandma, the family matriarch, did automatic writing and told people's futures. On one occasion, my older brother Harry became critically ill while visiting a family who lived on a farm in Indiana. Grandma had predicted his illness in her writings. When she got the message that he was ill, she insisted that my mom go to Indiana and rescue him. Mom brought him home for medical care, and he survived. Afterward, everyone said that Gran's warning had been instrumental in his survival.

My Aunt Marie was refined and always poised; she could read a person's future in the cards—Tarot, I believe. My mother, with her red-brown hair, high cheekbones, and deep-set hazel eyes, always knew before being told when someone in the family had died. She would see a vision of them appearing at her window, accompanied by an angel. Also, like her mother, she did automatic writing.

Mom had always been devoted to Christ but became deeply religious in her later years, though she rarely went to church. She had a large picture of Jesus in the living room and told people that the eyes followed you wherever you went. She once told me she saw Jesus riding on the hood of our car on a family trip. She was a simple, kind, and spiritually inclined person. In my earlier years, when Grandma lived with us, she was happy and a great mom.

Life on the farm was good for me—that is, until I was about five when my older brothers moved out due to a family squabble. My oldest brother was in the army, and my second brother was in high school when they left. I pleaded with them to stay, but they said they had to go. They didn't like my dad, who was, in fact, their stepdad. Then soon after they left, my grandmother started going to California for frequent, extended family visits.

After that, my days seemed long and lonely. I missed my brothers and my grandma. I still had my inner world with my animals and my imagination, but life wasn't the same. There were no big brothers to come home at night and play with me, and Grandma was always gone. I was suddenly an only child.

Then I got chicken pox in second grade and some kind of secondary condition. Finally, my doctor said I had an autoimmune problem and could not be around other children. I missed an entire year of school, and even though I had some tutoring, I still had to retake second grade the following year when we moved to Lombard.

Moving to the Sleepy Suburb

It wasn't that long after—I must have been around eight or nine—when we moved to a suburban house in a subdivision of Lombard. It was not country and not a town. Just houses and yards. It was a dry and arid place for me. My magical kingdom in nature was gone. My duck Jimmy was poisoned and died soon after we moved. My dog Pal died. Our chickens, our geese, and our pigs—all gone. I had only my cat in this empty place called a suburb.

For a while, we attended a Bible Church about four blocks away. My mother took me there occasionally, and we attended that church for about a year. We would walk in and sit in the pews, and soon the minister would go up front and give a rousing talk. People would get up and say they were saved and shout something like, "Thank you, Jesus," or, "Thank the Lord! I am saved." I would look at them, perplexed, wondering what on earth they were talking about. I couldn't figure it out. I didn't feel anything sacred there, though I kept thinking I should. I did not relate to this religion.

I did have a vivid imagination, though, and insatiable curiosity. In those days, I would ask my mother, "Why?" about all sorts of things. I wanted to know about everything. I think I annoyed her with my incessant questions. One night stands out in my memory. We were coming home from a church event.

My dad is driving. The stars are out and bright, sparkling with the cold. They are beautiful. You can see them crystal clear, the way you usually need to go to the mountains to view the stars. As we get out of our sedan, I stand in the cold night, breath frosting in the crisp air, and look up at the stars.

When my mom finishes packing up some things and gets out of the car, I ask her with all seriousness, "What happens to people

14

after they die?" She looks at me thoughtfully and then says, "I don't know. No one knows." I don't like her answer, so I tell her, "I'm going to find out when I grow up." I mean it. I am very sincere, so much so that I remember it to this day.

I was determined that I would be a person who knows the answers to this and other cosmic questions. Even in those early childhood days, questions about the nature of this existence consumed much of my thought. The rest was used for fantasy and play.

Moving to Town

Fortunately, we didn't stay in that sleepy neighborhood that was neither town nor country for too long. I believe I was in third grade when we moved into a neighboring town called Downers Grove. It was like moving out of a wasteland. The farm had been in Downers Grove too, but out in the country. Now we were in town, an outlying Chicago suburb with streets lined with stately maples and lovely older two-story homes.

Our new two-story house was about 125 years old, with gingerbread decorating it near the peak of the roof and a nice covered porch with a swing. It was only two blocks from downtown! I could walk to town. My elementary school—Lincoln—was also only a few blocks away. We remained in this house for the rest of my childhood and teens. This was to be my family home.

Moving into town was a breath of fresh air. I felt alive and excited to meet new friends and have new activities, but it still wasn't easy for me. Although I was much more at home in Downers Grove, I still struggled. My parents often argued, which upset me, but my biggest problem was that I felt different, not able to fit in. The other girls in school seemed to get all As and Bs. I got Cs and Ds in school and lots of demerits for poor posture and other things. I had to sit in a special row for the kids who got bad grades and were troublemakers. It was always all boys and me. The boys were often rowdy. I typically spent most of my days looking out the window and daydreaming.

When the teacher would call on me to read out loud, I would tense, knowing what a humiliating situation would follow. Reluctantly I would stand up and open the book; looking at the writing, I would begin to read, but somehow the letters would get mixed up. I would inevitably read the wrong word in a sentence and make all sorts of mistakes, reversing letters and even words. Finally, the teacher, obviously annoyed and frustrated with me, would be critical, and I, with a flushed face and lowered head, would sit down, ashamed. I didn't know about dyslexia then, and I am not sure my teachers did either. I only knew I was different and couldn't please the teachers like the other kids did—especially other girls.

I also needed help with fitting in socially. Social interactions were stressful for me. I felt different. I desperately wanted to be accepted by my little friends, but I was shy and embarrassed about my parents and my home. My parents did not belong to the PTA or do other socially acceptable parental things. We didn't have an immaculately clean house with plastic-covered furniture in our living room as my friends did. To me, we didn't fit—*I* didn't fit. It wasn't until some years later that I was able to acknowledge that I didn't like plastic-covered furniture or the superficial lifestyle that went along with it.

Even though I did not feel accepted at school and with the other kids, I knew there was more to me than people saw. I knew I was not stupid, and maybe my differentness was good. I called the world of human interactions the "people world," as opposed to my contemplative world, connected to nature with my trees, my cats, and my musings.

My physical appearance had changed by fourth grade. My hair had darkened to a deep auburn like my mom's and grandma's before me. I didn't have the family hazel eyes, but brown like my dad's. The color in my cheeks was always high. My hair was still long enough that I could sit on it. And I still had my freckles, though they had faded a bit.

I was a tall, gangly girl by then, almost five feet, towering over all my classmates. I often tried to slump down so I wouldn't stand out. But it didn't work. I felt like a giant and, along with my other differences, awkward. Yet I had friends and was involved in my school, where I wanted to fit in. By the fifth grade, I began to study people and copy what they did so that I could be acceptable to them.

This proved to be an effective tactic that worked at the time. I made friends, played with other kids, and had fun. We went to town together, played chase and hide games among the stores, and ran around town. We bought sodas at the local soda fountain and sat at the long wooden soda bar drinking root beer floats. We watched matinees at the local movie theater down the block and, in the winter, sledded down the hill that sloped from the water tower to our street. I melded into life as an ordinary child and enjoyed being a kid.

I didn't know at that time just how much and how soon my life would change, and my spiritual calling quicken. At the time, I also failed to realize how mimicking others kept me from bringing forward who I truly was. Instead, I outwardly became what others wanted so that I might be a part of their "people world." It took me years to realize the extent to which I was hiding my spiritual inclinations, ideas, and visions from others in order to fit in and be what others wanted. In this process, I lost sight of something essential, the ability to live a life that truly expresses my being openly in the world. It was not until many years later that I had to confront this pattern of hiding while appearing to be an open person. When I finally did, my life changed dramatically.

Grandmother's Leaving

Around sixth grade, at twelve or thirteen, my childhood happiness was interrupted by the death of my grandmother, who was like a second mother to me. Her passing was celebrated by a grand Irish wake, befitting the cultured Irish lady and Gaelic singer, the matriarch of the family that she was. There must have been at least 500 people at her wake.

The twelve children and their families (there were a bunch of us!) stayed together for three days during the wake, everyone dressed in black, going in and out viewing the body at the funeral home during the day and attending big rollicking family dinners together in the evenings. In the back parlor of the home where my Gran was laid out, my uncles sat smoking cigars and telling jokes, and everyone laughed and ate their fill. But everyone inside missed Grandma and cried when they went to view her body.

After her passing, as with many extended families of the time, our larger family visits began to fade. Also, around this time, things began to stir inside for me, and my spirit awaken, moving up the first rung of the triangle of the destiny I had seen when I was younger.

Chapter II
First Openings

I had always thrived around trees and animals. I understood them. When I felt upset and in turmoil because of social pressures in the "people world" and the tensions at home, I would go outside and find the trees on my block that I had a connection with. Taking my distress to them, I would go to one of my trees and hug it. When I did this, a warm glow would surround me; my body relaxing, as if a burden had been lifted from my shoulders. The turmoil and upset would float away like clouds, to be replaced by a serene calmness that came from the tree. I felt a genuine friendship with these trees. It seemed I could communicate with them. The calm order in their minds and their sense of self was understandable to me.

I knew that they could also sense me, and my awareness of their minds. In this way, we communicated—not like people communicate, but in the slow rhythm of trees. I found the minds of trees to be very different from people's minds. The trees shared with me from being to being, and certain trees then knew me, and I knew them. We were friends. They cared for me. In times of need, when I turned to them, these trees would heal me in friendship.

Animals, like trees, wove friendships with me from my youngest years onward. It seemed they knew me and opened their minds to me. I could feel them the same way I could feel the trees. Holding them or being near them, I knew when I connected with them how the world looked and felt from their perspective. Being with them, it was as if I was looking out of their eyes, feeling their feeling of being themselves, feeling their urges, their interests as they arose, knowing life from their viewpoint. It may be a kind of empathy that remains with me to this day—and connects me to living beings.

When I hit my early teens, things quickened. For the first time, I began to be aware of people's consciousness, much as I had for years with animals and trees. Of course, it was much different, as people's minds seemed very different from animals or trees. When I would meet someone, before I would begin talking with them, I could see their mind in my mind, almost like a kind of flow chart.

I could see that on deeper levels, we were all much alike. Then I would see fundamental complexes held in different people's minds, such as inferiority or superiority. Over that, I would see other complexes built upon these, but much more individualized to the person, less universal. The vision would continue until the other person would speak and shatter my observations with the sound of their voice. Once I began interacting, the lay of their mind would slip from my view.

This experience of observing the structure of other people's minds frequently happened during my early teens, but it then faded. I never spoke of it to anyone, as no one around me would understand. I lived in a very superficial world, and those around me were more concerned with simple, external interests.

In retrospect, I do not think I was as alone as I thought I was in my belief that I was different. As it turned out, many youths of my generation shared this perception. Looking back, I think perhaps we came here to be a force of change. Most kids are self-conscious to some extent, but I really didn't fit. I had to fight for my identity against a society that focused on the superficial and did not recognize the non-material.

A Mysterious Holy Presence

My first experience of divine grace happened when a mysterious holy presence came to me at around twelve or thirteen. This was my first encounter with the *Guru* (guide) of my life, whom I later came to know as my Baba. However, I would not know that name until many years later.

During my early teens, when I was distressed or crying, a subtle, comforting presence began to weave itself into the edges of my awareness. As I paid attention to it, I sensed this to be the holy presence of a great being. This presence seemed distinctly male and God-like. I don't know exactly when he first came to me, but it was around the same time as my grandmother's passing or just before it.

When I would be upset and my mind distressed, this compassionate presence would surround me and emanate love, diffusing feelings of difficulty. The struggles in my mind would fall away. I would find myself melting into a safe, kind comfort flowing from this unknown presence. Mysterious, he never gave a name, though I knew him more deeply than I had ever known anyone in this life. He would come to me as a silent companion. I recall one time, though there were many back then.

It is night. I am sitting on the front porch of our home, feeling a powerful, divine Presence come near to me. The full moon is bathing the porch in moonlight while I sit, gently rocking on the swing. Aware of the loneliness of my life, I feel this compassionate, comforting presence settling next to me. The presence never speaks but is simply with me, as he often is when I need help. I know him as a feeling, a sense of another, a very caring, wise being. There is no guidance or teaching from this presence, only comforting awareness of his nearness to me and of his love.

At some point, I come to feel that this Presence and I have been together before, somewhere. Somewhere different than here. I begin to remember another time, another place where I am with this one, whom I think of as my Lord. I belong there, where this Presence is a physical person. I see myself with him, though I cannot see the forms. It was a world of forests and ways that were more harmonious with nature. A world with very different values than the one I am growing up in. A world where people knew that trees are living beings and people knew that they are a part of the whole and value the whole.

The world I am growing up in seems alien to me. It appears in my child's mind as if people's values are upside down and confused. It feels like a strange world, and I am a stranger in it. I begin to think that perhaps I am being punished for some failure by being made to come here and live without him in this land where I feel so out of place, so different. It seems to me that I must have done something wrong to deserve to be in this place. I think this, yet I sense from the Presence that this is untrue. I am not here because I am being punished for some failure. As painful as it is, that is not the reason I am here, physically separated from my divine Beloved.

I cannot explain this feeling of previous physical closeness in a different time and place and the present physical separation I experienced. Although I had no concept of reincarnation and would not be exposed to this idea until many years later, still, this was my experience. Rationally, in the framework I knew, it made no sense. But children are not always rational.

There was a pain in my heart that he was not a physical person, someone I could touch or talk to. He was not a part of the world I lived in. Many long nights I cried myself to sleep; many lonely hours I longed for him and a very different world that I remembered. One night, as a young girl of perhaps twelve, I could bear the separation no longer, so I slipped out of my house in the wee hours of the night.

I emerge from my house. The moon is bright, and the feeling of my divine Companion comes to me. I begin to walk, the silent Presence beside me. For hours this invisible holy Presence and I walk together through the town with its shuttered buildings and stores closed for the night, then miles more along the train tracks where grass grows up wild amid the rails. The summer night smells of fresh-cut grasses and honeysuckle waft on a gentle breeze as I walk and walk miles from home.

He walks next to me, along the rails, in moonlight so bright it seems almost daytime. I walk with him till the wee hours of the morning. He is not visible to my eyes, but I can see him with a kind of inner sight. Vaguely I sense a form near me. He is not tall or stout. It seems he is dressed in white. I walk, and I talk to him in my mind. He does not answer with words but somehow does through the touch of his mere presence.

After the walk, he sits with me, in this ephemeral form, swinging on the porch until almost sunrise. I am deeply in love.

Trying to Understand

I had no reference to any such being existing except for Jesus in the Bible. Trying to understand my experience and this being my only reference, after some time, I began to identify the presence I sensed as God or perhaps Jesus. Reading about Christ, I thought, "This must be the one I have met. He is like him." So, though he never gave a name, after a while, I came to assume this mysterious presence must be Christ.

With this idea came a passionate love for Jesus. I felt a tremendous longing, crying because I was 2,000 years too late. The one I remembered was gone from this earth, or so I thought, leaving me with heart-breaking grief that I had missed him and lived in this age, in this society as it was then, dry: no mysticism, no miracles, no beloved, compassionate, God-like Beings. Only kids playing, school, growing up, and getting married. I did not find out until much later how mistaken I was to assume this holy Presence I loved so deeply was unreachable, gone from this world.

The Hill and the Cosmos

At the end of our block in Downers Grove was a hill. It was, for that area, a good-sized hill. All the kids sledded down it in winter. On its apex rested a water tower, which made the hill public property rather than someone's yard. It was a grassy hill, and as it wasn't private, it was a place I could go and be alone. One profoundly moving summer night on this hill stands out clearly in my memory, for it changed my life.

It is evening, after school. I am in seventh grade and beset by the turmoil and emotional anguish that often occurs from the stress of relating to the "people world." I wait until it is late in the evening, after dark. Then I leave the house and walk up the hill at the end of our street to a grassy area near the old water tower. I find a spot where I can see the stars clearly and sit down on the grass, touching it with my hands as I sit back. The grass is cool and dry, not covered with dew, so I lie down on this plush green carpet to gaze up at the night sky.

The stars are magnificent. Crystal clear and abundant. Looking up, I begin to imagine how far it is to the moon, to the sun, to the stars. I begin to imagine a distance of one mile, then of a hundred miles, of a thousand, a million miles, to envision the vastness of the universe and to feel the beautiful and perfect order of the cosmos. In my mind, I see the planets revolving around the sun, a multitude of stars, and untold numbers of living beings, all existing in a vast, interwoven, interconnected web of life. I envision solar systems within galaxies of countless suns, woven into the order and peace of this vast universe.

Slowly I begin to envision the molecular and atomic levels as well, seeing the beautiful harmony and order that exists there. My mind's eye perceives the orderly process of subatomic particles circling, each in their energy field, moved by forces in perfect sync with all that is. I realize how the cosmos is a vast and orderly flow from the smallest to the most expansive; that Earth itself and the natural world are part of this harmony.

With this insight, I become aware that the turmoil and chaos I experience in my life only exist in a small spectrum of creation that encompasses human society, the human mind, and my mind. My sense of being a stranger in a strange land, out of place, loses importance. Life is all right because the universe is intact, in eternal peace and harmony.

This realization gives me great comfort. My sense of confusion and chaos with this odd world I live in floats away. I am oriented again. I begin to realize that everything that is happening is okay. It doesn't matter how much pain and chaos there is in my life if the universe is as it should be. With a sense of joy, I see that this world is just a small bandwidth in which chaos exists. The rest of the cosmos is in perfect order. There is a deep sense of relief in this realization.

With this experience, life began to make more sense to me and to have a context. I think there were many visits to this hill, many nights spent with just me and the stars, the moon, my trees, and, of course, the mysterious

God-like Presence that visited me. The stars and cosmos, the earth, this ordered, harmonious universe I came to recognize as my mother and this loving God-like Presence as my father. This realization was not simply an idea. It was core for me. I loved the mysterious, divine Presence I thought of as my father and found my comfort in him, as well as the universe around me—the trees with their calm, quiet minds, and my animal friends—my divine mother.

Alone

As I have said, I did not share these experiences with other people. I was afraid friends wouldn't understand and would reject me, so I continued to fit into the "people world" by being what others wanted. However, inside I felt different and didn't want others to know how different I was.

By late childhood and early teens, I would spend hours alone, trying to understand the world around me. At times I would sit in our upstairs library by the window, looking out and contemplating why people act as they do in different situations. I would wonder, and I would discover. I would come up with my own theories about how the mind works and what motivates action, incorporating my intuitive observations of people. I would also contemplate other topics, such as the nature of trees and animals' minds, the relationships of living beings, and similar issues regarding the nature of our existence.

I was aware that my family and the other children that I knew had no such thoughts. I felt invisible to those around me. I desperately wanted to share myself with others and be close to them, but there was no one with whom I could honestly share.

Once I approached my mother, who was perhaps the most accessible to my world of anyone I knew. I explained to her some ideas I had come up with about how people use defenses to justify themselves and about superiority and inferiority complexes. Sharing my ideas was a very personal disclosure since I was not prone to discuss my thoughts with others. My mother looked at me with a clear and complete lack of comprehension. She simply did not know what I was talking about. I was a child, and children do not talk like that. My mother was not intellectually inclined, nor was anyone in my family. She made some simple comments indicating her lack of comprehension and interest.

I never again tried to communicate my experiences to those around me while I was growing up, as it was clear to me that they would not understand. However, I did find acknowledgment eventually in my studies as I grew older. Once in my senior year in high school, I happened upon the very theories I had attempted to explain to my mother in a textbook on psychology. Slowly, as I grew, I became less and less alone, and the realizations of my childhood were confirmed.

Forgetting

This deeply internal life of late childhood was a solitary mystical exploration. However, I desired human connection and involvement, and so I became more social. Somewhere in my early teens, I began to give up and forget my feelings of destiny and the presence that comforted me. I became extroverted at this point in my life and my sweet, divine friend of childhood seemed remote and unreachable. He faded from my mind. I began to think it was only a dream, a childhood fantasy. I turned to the world to lose myself, as I did not know how to find my destiny.

By around fourteen, I experienced a momentous change. I was now officially a teenager and attending eighth grade. My life turned around. I discovered boys, dating, and friendships. I began to live on the outside of my experiences. My desire to be happy and accepted by friends in the world I lived in pulled me outwards. My school grades went up. People stopped caring if I could spell. I was acceptable. My life was my school, my boyfriends, and my friends.

Visiting Churches

My spiritual journey also became extroverted. I wanted to find the truth, and so I decided in my mid-teens to go to various churches to find the true way. I became active with the Episcopal church and went through confirmation. But I could not find my Beloved there, so I began to attend a Baptist church to see if this fundamentalist religion contained the truth. But I also could not find what

31

I searched for there. I sang the hymns, attended the services, and searched for God. But I could not find him there. Then I tried a Congregational church and, finally, a church youth group in which I found great friendships, a boy I loved, and many good times. But not serious spirituality.

Finally, I recall, at perhaps fifteen, sitting alone in a church near my parents' house. I sat on a bench in one of the pews, in empty rows, in an empty church, and opened a hymn book. I began to contemplate my experience and the search I had made in recent years for God. My earlier experiences from childhood were now distant. I looked through the hymn book, reading the words of different hymns. I had searched, but I had not found. I began to think of the suffering in the world, of the hollowness I felt in the churches. I began to think that perhaps we have created God. I began to believe there is no God, or at least I could not find him. The words in the hymns rang hollow. I closed the book and decided I had searched for him in vain—for something that wasn't there.

Being a Beatnik

And so, I forgot about God and became a young beatnik. I wore black, quoted Allen Ginsberg, sang folk songs, wrote poetry, read Erich Fromm, and believed in existentialism. I admired arty movies, joined the civil rights movement, and spent my free time in coffee houses and riding in my boyfriend's red Ferrari convertible. At sixteen, I was an intellectual, rejecting the society I grew up in and its values.

In high school, I liked being different. I was part of a group of beatniks, and I truly enjoyed my offbeat community of friends. This was a time of existentialism in my life. We spoke of the meaning and meaninglessness of life. We sang it in folk songs. We tried marijuana and enjoyed it. We liked to defy society. We disrespected and openly rebelled against the superficial society we had grown up in. We challenged its values at every turn. But when it came time for college, we all turned in our applications, took advantage of the affluence we scorned, and went off to school.

First Years in College

I went to college in Southern Illinois at a school that had a reputation as a party school. It took me less than a school quarter to discover that this school lived up to its reputation. I do not know how I managed to keep my grades up in my first year, as I spent most of my time drinking and attending wild parties. The external black of my beatnik years was gone, and social events dominated my life.

My search for God became instead a search for true love with the man of my dreams. In fact, from junior high through my first college year, I believe that I searched for the true love of my childhood in all the various boys I fell madly in love with. In each one, I tried to find my true happiness. When relationships broke up, I was shattered. But then I would quickly find a new love of my life, always longing for the deepest, most intense love I could find. Sexually I was conservative, but emotionally I was passionate and romantic.

Then as the hippie movement came into full bloom, I discovered I was a hippie, a radical, and a students' rights protestor. By my second year in college, I had dropped out and dropped in. By the end of my second year, I had met my first husband, been teargassed in student protests, rediscovered smoking weed, and found LSD. I dressed in psychedelic paisley and bell-bottom pants, ironed my long auburn hair to straighten my wavy curls, and stayed up stoned all night painting canvases with surrealistic images for my art classes. I thought that if only the whole world, and the powers that be, would turn on and tune in, there would be no more war. They would discover love, as I had, and the world's problems would be over.

Chapter III
Psychedelic Awakening

*A*s I continued down the road of psychedelics, I entered a period in my life that was to change me forever. I was twenty-two and now lived in a house off campus with my soon-to-be husband, Jack, and two good friends of ours, Jerry and Michael. Jerry was a tall blond man, very bright, with an odd sense of humor, and Michael was an intellectual Black artist from the East Coast who sported a great afro and wild ideas. My husband-to-be was a medium-built man with long, sandy-colored hair, a big handlebar mustache, and a kind demeanor. He loved to smoke pot and tell crazy stories. We were all students at the university, artists, and stoners.

We enjoyed getting high on weed, being creative, and just having fun. Jack and I and a few friends would often smoke some weed and go for long late-night walks on hot Southern Illinois summer nights. Contemplating society, the universe, and everything, we solved the problems of the world by walking, talking, and laughing. I had forgone my first-year drunken party school for this hippie lifestyle and a close group of friends I liked.

As in the Beatnik days of my high school years, we were not only stoners but intellectual radicals and artists, bucking the system. When the war protests began, I joined SDS (Students for a Democratic Society), fought for student rights and against the war, watched friends get arrested in the middle of the night and taken to faraway jails for protesting, and eventually, saw our roommate Michael leave for Canada in protest to the draft. This was the time just before Kent State when student riots were in full swing.

From the Summer of Love through these turbulent times, getting high, tripping, and being flower children was what we were all about. And somehow, despite dropping out and dropping in, we all managed to go to school and get college educations while focusing on getting stoned, listening to acid rock, and being hippies. In fact, Jerry went on to become a noted psychologist, and Michael distinguished himself as an artist in France. And as for me, I managed, through my spiritual quest with LSD and all that followed, to continue my studies and eventually get a Ph.D. And Jack—well, Jack was Jack. Eventually, he became a social worker.

This was a shifting time of change in the world when an entire generation awoke from the slumber of middle-class material life to mind-altering substances, music, and new ideas while standing up against a war. This crazy scene was the backdrop for two years of my journey of spirit, a psychedelic journey of awakening beyond my wildest dreams.

Rediscovering God

The journey took off when one day, a friend of mine told me she was going to take LSD, along with some other people who were at the house. She asked if I wanted to join them, and I said, "Sure! Why not." I was always open to getting high. So, she handed me this little capsule, and I swallowed it. It took a while to kick in—and then things started to change. This first trip was an entirely new experience for me. Way more out there than smoking weed.

Once things got going and the whole place was undulating in waves of colors, the group decided to leave the house and go for a walk. What did I know? They took me by the hand, and I just went along. On the walk, I got all turned around about where I was and how to return to the house, but it was okay. It was fun, colorful, and trippy. There were moments when I would stare at something and lose myself in wonder and unity, dissolving into bliss.

Then I would return and enjoy the colors and textures of things I saw as if I had never really seen them before. Everything around me became more alive, more vital than I had ever known it to be. Eyes wide and dilated, face lit with wonder, I explored this amazing reality around me. The group led me around on this trippy excursion. I just followed, which was about all I was capable of. Eventually, we somehow made it home. That was my first experience. It was great, opening new dimensions— yet it was only the beginning.

After a few trips on LSD, I discovered a book by Timothy Leary called *The Psychedelic Experience*. It described my experiences and became a kind of bible for me as I entered a self-charted path into the unknown, using psychedelics to go deeper and deeper into an exploration of the farther reaches of consciousness. I read Timothy Leary and experienced every word in the very fiber of my being. Taking LSD, I traveled through the universe and found all beings to be one Being, all creation an expression of love. I was not a small and separate person. I discovered I was One, in ecstatic union with all existence. I would lie on the floor, listening to acid rock music—feeling merged into the very core of existence.

I had forgotten God, forgotten the divine Presence I thought of as my father of childhood and my feelings about the universe as my divine mother. I had forgotten, lost in my external life—until I discovered LSD. With it, the world unraveled before me. I was immersed in love. Time slowed down, and infinity came into view.

I would pick up a leaf and look into it, and I would go into the molecular order of the microcosm. At the same time, my mind would go out into the vastness of the heavens, expanding in both directions until the infinite smallness of the microcosm and the infinite vastness of the macrocosm became lost in that which is beyond words, beyond time, beyond space. I would be lost in an experience that has no name, no person, no time, no beginning, and no end. Then slowly, the universe would begin to re-form, and again, I would exist, still holding a leaf in my hand.

My mind filled with awe and love, and I discovered God. I discovered that which I had always wanted. I thought I had found the door and I was in heaven when I was on LSD. Deep feelings of my union with all existence pervaded my trips. I was in ecstasy beyond my wildest dreams. The universe was made of love, and I could explore it fully with my mind. Donovan spoke to me: "Fly Trans-Love Airways, get you there on time."

On the light side of these experiences, I would laugh and share visions with my roommate Jerry. We often tripped together. He would lean back in his big, over-stuffed recliner and point out different-colored bubbles on the ceiling. Laughing, he would say, "Hey, look at that one!"

I would look up, and I could see it too! With wonder in my voice, I would reply, "Far out, wow, that's amazing!" And after a bit of letting my mind spin into infinity and getting lost for a time in the space between now and then, I would come back and point, "Hey, look over there. You see that yellow one?"

"Yeah, I can see it!" Jerry would exclaim as he sat back and laughed, and I laughed with him as the universe unfolded around us.

But it was not fun that kept me taking LSD. I had found what I had always searched for. I had found my Beloved in the impartial form of cosmic love in these intense, all-pervading experiences. In subjective time, each of my psychedelic experiences seemed to last almost a full human lifetime. Though in the outer world, a session would be only 10 or 12 hours, in the inner world, time seemed to slow—and each experience lasted many, many years, a lifetime. Due to these experiences on LSD, I feel as if I have had the opportunity to live many lives in subjective time within this one small lifetime.

As I continued my deep dive into the exploration of consciousness on LSD, each trip began to build one upon another. I would often experience my environment molecularly, literally seeing the molecular patterns and union of all existence. Waves would come where I would merge completely and then re-form my existence. Time would move very, very slowly in the heart of the experience, and I would be lost in the union, merged with the absolute love which is the nature of all that is.

There was a pattern to this. On each trip, I went progressively deeper into consciousness. As I did, time would slow down proportionately, and the bliss of being in unitary wholeness would grow deeper. I would dissolve into the One and be filled with love and bliss. Then time would slow and slow again to barely moving as my immersion deepened. Lifetimes would go by, immersed in love unbound. After a seemingly endless time, slowly, I would begin to emerge from this state, time picking up its pace, my mind re-forming. My persona would come back into existence. I would return to normalized time and the experience of a separate existence that I had grown up thinking of as reality.

This transition after a trip was difficult for me. It was extremely painful to lose the experience of this love and to know that I could not hold it except on a drug. The gap between the unitary spiritual reality during my psychedelic experiences and daily life in duality was wide. Mundane worldly existence did not hold what I wanted. I wanted the union with all that is, unfettered love. Between trips, I would grow restless and discontent. After a few painful weeks of separation from that which was dear to me, again, I would take LSD and melt my being into absolute love.

Experiencing the Unmanifest

As I continued this journey of the soul, using LSD as my doorway to mystical realms, a day came when my experience reached its apex and forever changed me. As I have mentioned, with each LSD trip, a deeper and deeper experience of ecstatic union occurred and, along with it, a parallel slowing of time. The experience of the ecstatic union of all things reached a progressively more profound depth as I continued my exploration. This went on for some time, perhaps a year or two. Then I took the trip, which I experienced as fully opening the door into the universe and forever closing it for psychedelics. It remains clear in my mind as if happening today.

I have taken the magic capsule, and reality is altering. As is the usual pattern, time is slowing, the experience of love and union unfolding. It deepens as before, and time becomes ever so slow with almost no movement. I lie on my bed, lost in the experience, unable to move. The feelings of love and union are total. I lose awareness of myself as a person. Deep ecstatic feelings are in full bloom when suddenly, like breaking through a membrane, or a dimensional veil, the ecstatic unitary love simply ceases.

Piercing the veil, time seems to stop. I am not a person with a body. That is long gone. I am aware. My awareness, or should I simply say "Awareness," follows a singular point of light through a kind of void. Then this light pierces another veil of some kind. In that instant, the universe—the entire, vast, manifest universe—flashes before me or before awareness, and a singular, stunning realization reverberates throughout. "I have created all of this. It never existed in the first place!"

With this stunning realization, I see planets, solar systems, galaxies, and universes folding into themselves. All manifest existence folds into itself, implodes, and ceases to be. Time absolutely stops. There is no time, no space, no movement, and no bliss. There is only awareness, consciousness, a knowingness wavering between existence and non-existence.

I would say this is a void, but a void is something, and this is awareness without an object. The manifest universe is gone, truly gone. The experience does not seem like an illusion. It seems very real, more real than anything I have ever known. I cannot say it is appealing or that it is not appealing. It simply is, unmanifest, without attribute, something between existence and non-existence. And then even knowing is gone. Beyond that, there is no memory.

Then, somehow, I am back. I exist again in the experience of bliss and unitary wholeness. Time, although moving very slowly, is again in motion. The union I experience is blissful but doesn't feel correct. There is confusion. One experience and then the other is strange for me. I had been unformed. I do not know why or how I am again formed. I experience a fundamental contradiction. All of this was gone. I was gone. How can I be here? How is time moving, and I am back in this body, in this little life? I cannot understand. There is this feeling, this sense that I have ceased to be and should not be here again.

Then, after some time, the experiences of union and love also begin to decrease in intensity, and time begins to pick up movement, as in past experiences, but I cannot shake the discomfort I feel, as if I have reentered reality at a slight tilt. The basic contradiction makes me unsettled.

I know inside that I can never reach these states again on LSD. I know instinctually that psychedelics have done what they were meant to do, and I can never open the door again. As the LSD slowly wears off and I return to my normal waking consciousness, I know very clearly: this path is closed.

A Door Closes & A Fall from Grace

In my heart, I wanted to immerse myself in this universal love I had discovered on psychedelics. My daily life as a student at the university, as a small and separate person, was shabby indeed compared to these visionary experiences. At that time in my life, I thought these altered states of universal love and consciousness were something produced by a substance. Intuitively I knew the psychedelic door was closed, but I had no other means to access the experiences, so I took LSD again. I had a devastating trip. Instead of opening the door to union with the Universe, fear opened like a bottomless pit and devoured me.

Panic arose. I could not experience love and felt trapped in my separateness and terror. I took a major tranquilizer to try to end the experience that, after much time and much pain, slowly subsided. I was shaken by my first "bad trip," but I still longed for the union and ecstatic love I'd once had. I wanted this so badly that, despite knowing this door was closed, I again tried LSD a few weeks later.

Again, it opened terror within me. Again, I could not reach unity and love and became trapped in separateness and fear. During this LSD experience, a drug-crazed man lunged at me and raised waves of unbearable fear. That night a pain started in my lower back, and my back began to tighten in an arch. I could not control this. I had never heard of *kundalini* at the time, so I had no idea what was going on. My husband held me through the night. The drug wore off, but the fear, the terror that had opened like an abyss, did not go away.

For months afterward, I could not reach past separateness and fear. I clutched in terror at my husband, hugging him. But all I could see was that he was only made of flesh and blood, that his existence was transitory and not solid. I realized he could not make me safe. I grasped at anything, anyone, to save me from this fear, this pit of terror I had entered.

The world around me seemed a semi-transparent existence. When I looked, things I thought were solid before no longer seemed as if they could support my being. I could see that everything in this world is transitory and insubstantial. I realized that this world is ephemeral and passing. It could not save me, could not give me true shelter. I grasped, but all I had previously thought made me safe and secure slipped through my fingers like water. Nothing could shelter me from fear, or so I thought at that time. I did not know how to get out of the terror. I saw myself teetering on the edge of a vast, unfathomable precipice, a black nothingness I was about to fall into. The existential void I had bantered about in my teens had become a stark reality for me.

Unlike the love and union on psychedelics or even the dissolution of creation, this existential void terrified me. I did not know anyone to whom this had happened. It was not until many years later that I learned that this experience of the insubstantial nature of material reality is often a part of the mystic path. Mystics of many traditions have written about the insubstantial nature of this world, but I had never read those mystics or even heard of them. It was a fragile time for me when I entered this existential void, and I needed careful guidance to pass through. Yet I had no guidance, no one who understood. I had to transit this truth the hard way.

I knew I needed help, so I found a psychiatrist a friend had told me about and went to see him. Desperately afraid to be alone for even a moment, I asked my husband Jack, to go with me. We went to the doctor's office and sat in the waiting room. I was called in and sat on the other side of a large desk in front of the doctor. When I told my story and described my fear, this self-confident and somewhat self-important man declared that my problem was due to drugs. He told me that if I had not been a rebel, if I had not taken psychedelics but had simply led a nice, middle-class life, I would not be in this pain.

He spent his time with me pointing out that everything I stood for was wrong, that all my dreams and visions of the Divine were worthless, and that I had better follow the straight and narrow path. Then, perhaps, if I was lucky, I might improve. He clearly did not think much of me. He wanted me to set my goal to lead a middle-class life and never to chase after ecstatic visions. It was all nonsense to him. And after all, look at the trouble it had landed me in.

After seeing him, I was defeated and in despair of the worst kind. I had thrown caution to the wind and reached for my heart's desire. And I had failed miserably. I was broken, constricted. Trapped in fears of insanity and feelings of separateness, the experiences of love and divine union seemed out of reach. My heart was broken.

In this defeated state, I was afraid to be alone. I needed people desperately. In my dependency, I was deeply grateful for whatever kindness anyone would show to me. But I felt like a parasite. Crippled and needy, I could help no one, only take whatever people were kind enough to give.

I was young, perhaps 22. My life was ahead of me, but to me, this life looked like a prison sentence given for my mental inadequateness. I blamed myself. I remember going to a store and standing with other people thinking, "All my life I have wanted to help others, but I am in such need I can only take. I have nothing to give. It would be better if I were dead. Then I wouldn't be a burden on anyone."

A Turning Point

Broken, dependent, plagued by feelings of terror, and afraid to be alone, I held a very low opinion of myself. I thought I was on the verge of insanity. I quit all drugs, including smoking cigarettes, and continued in school as I didn't know what else to do.

Then the next semester, I took a course in Eastern philosophy. It was an elective, and I thought it might be interesting. Toward the beginning of the coursework, the teacher gave us the assignment to read the *Bhagavad Gita*. It looked like a somewhat large text, so I wasn't enthused about it. But when I began to read, I was amazed! I could hardly believe what I was reading! In it, they were speaking about the exact experiences I'd had on LSD! How could this be?

The realization began to dawn on me that these states I had experienced must exist apart from drugs. I began to realize that the understandings I had reached, the love and unity, were not simply drug-induced hallucinations. People living thousands of years ago had the same experiences, and they did not take drugs. I realized that my visions were real, and that which I treasured in my heart actually existed! I had lived for many months heartbroken, in complete darkness. Now a ray of hope, a light, entered my darkness.

Krishna, in the *Bhagavad Gita,* reminded me of the childhood presence I had known. In the *Gita,* Krishna tells Arjuna, "I am ever present to those who have realized me in every creature. Seeing all life as my manifestation, they are never separated from me." Then he says to Arjuna that all existence abides in divine union with the infinite *Brahma.* "My highest nature, the imperishable Brahma, gives every creature its existence and lives in every creature." When I read this, I understood it and knew it to be the truth.

Then in the Gita, Krishna shows Arjuna his true form. "Behold, Arjuna, a million divine forms with an infinite variety of colors and shapes...behold the cosmos turning within my body.... If a thousand suns were to rise in the heavens at the same time, the blaze of their light would resemble the splendor of that supreme spirit." "Arjuna then saw all the manifest forms of the universe united as one..." The book went on to explain the amazing cosmic existence of Krishna, and I knew, I knew I had found my home again, my way.

I came to realize that the holy Presence that had cared for me as a child, and the visions I had been given on LSD, were not some deluded fantasies but the grace of the immortal, infinite, Divine One. The cosmic Self of all beings has a way of guiding and taking care of those who seek to know, even when they stumble over themselves and fall. This was my first brush with the great wisdom of the East.

From reading the Gita, I came to understand that meditation is the path to this vision I so loved. The psychedelic door was closed, but now there was another door. Through it, the union I longed for could be attained without hallucinogens and become a lasting experience. I wanted this.

Yet I felt fearful after my last efforts. How could I do meditation? After all, the psychiatrist had told me I should stop chasing crazy visions of love and unitary consciousness and settle for an ordinary life.

However, as time went on, I could not resist the desire to begin meditation. One day my husband Jack said to me, "Hey, let's drive up to Wheaton and see the Theosophical Society. They have their main center there. We can stay at your parents' house." Wheaton is near Downers Grove, about a five-hour drive north.

I thought about it and answered, "Yeah, okay, that could be interesting. I hear they have some cool esoteric books and stuff on magic. Also, maybe there's something on meditation I can get."

About a week later, we loaded up our old white Chevy and headed up for Wheaton, Illinois, I in my paisley bell bottoms with hair blowing in the breeze from the open windows and Jack with his long hair, handlebar mustache, and Indiana Jones hat. When we got there, we were duly impressed. The place was really cool, with an amazing metaphysical library. We stayed for hours looking through all their fascinating books.

I bought a book from them on meditation. I figured I'd take the leap and try it, but when I got home and started reading the book, it said you should not meditate without a Guru, and that it could be dangerous. I knew about dangerous, but really! A Guru! We lived in the middle of nowhere! In Southern Illinois! There were no meditation teachers or Gurus around. No one meditated. Where was I going to find a Guru?

After a few months, my desire to meditate surpassed my fear, and I thought, "I will begin meditation on my own, as there is no teacher." I started meditation practices on my own, and as fate would have it—or maybe some of that cosmic grace I had been learning about—within a week, much to my amazement, two meditation teachers showed up in Carbondale, of all places—the backwaters of Southern Illinois!

This was the beginning of some amazing synchronicities that started to occur. One speaker was a Transcendental Meditation teacher and the other was an Indian monk in orange robes from an Eastern yoga and meditation group. He had come to SIU because the only person he knew in the entire United States was an Indian man who was living in Carbondale and attending the university. I don't know why, but I was only drawn to see the monk. Somehow it felt like the real deal, and when I did see him, the philosophy he talked about fit in with Bucky (Buckminster) Fuller's work.

Even with my internal struggles, I managed to graduate from college and then enter grad school in the Department of Design, where I began to study with Bucky, who is most famous for his work with geodesic domes. But I was interested in his ideas about how to make the world work for all humanity, a program he called "World

Game," and one world government. I became a teaching assistant for Bucky as part of my graduate studies.

Bucky always said that the triangle is the basic structure of the universe. And this monk, who called himself *Dadaji*, a Sanskrit term meaning brother, basically said the same thing and explained ideas that supported my understanding of the cosmos. Everything he said fit in with my experiences and with what I knew to be true. So, I was all in after seeing him and asked this Dadaji to teach me meditation.

The Bhagavad Gita, translated by Eknath Easwaran, Nilgiri Press 1985

Chapter IV
The Path Unfolds

*I*n 1969 I became initiated into the Eastern yogic meditation path that Dadaji was teaching. I was very happy. A light was shining in my life, a hope that I could once again find the blissful wholeness I so loved. I started doing regular meditation twice daily, as Dadaji had advised, and I attended group meditations and retreats. It was great! But within a few months, I began to have unusual experiences.

I would see the color purple in meditation, and I would hear sounds from far away. Unusual body sensations began to occur during my meditations, such as a feeling my head being very large, or my body turned to one side or oversized. Then one day, while doing my yoga postures, I sensed what I thought was the Guru's presence and thought I heard him speaking to me.

Already worried about my mental stability, I did not necessarily welcome these unusual experiences, especially since no one else seemed to be having them. So, I went to see Dadaji to ask for advice. We had a meeting, and I told him what had been happening in my meditations. He listened and simply said it was all in my imagination and that I should forget about it. My cheeks flushed, and I lowered my head, deeply embarrassed and hurt when he told me this. I then thanked him and withdrew.

I knew that I had mental issues, or at least I thought I did, and, at the time, it was clear to me that this must be the reason these unusual experiences were happening to me and not to others. It was not until many years later that I understood that these and similar experiences happen to people when meditation opens subtle spheres. But at the time, I didn't know this. After talking to Dada, feelings of discouragement and dejection arose for me. Ashamed and feeling unworthy, I became afraid to meditate. Although I wanted nothing more than to meditate and potentially feel unity again, I stopped my practices.

Three or four months passed before I slowly regained a small amount of self-confidence and timidly began to try meditation again. This time nothing unusual happened. Everything was quite normal, and my experience was just like everyone else's. This reassured me, so I was able to continue practicing—and everything began to look up.

Miracles Begin

However, unusual events began to happen in my life. Jack and I were students, but we rented a farm outside of Carbondale where we had gotten married and were living. We loved it there. We were back-to-nature hippies by that time. Then one day, we came home, and as if out of nowhere, we received an eviction notice from our landlord.

We had to move. Soon. Jack went to the student housing office to get a housing list—not a very good place to find a farm like the one we had—but the only place we knew to look. To our amazement, there was a farm listed on it for rent. This was unusual, as farms were at a premium and always rented.

However, the listing was several weeks old, so we did not even bother to call, as we thought it would already be rented. I called all the other listings instead. Unfortunately, everything was rented. I could find nothing. A week or so later, I noticed the list lying on our table and, although I was sure it was useless, decided to call the farm number. An older Southern Illinois gentleman answered and, in a thick Southern drawl, told me that he and his sister did have a house to rent on their farm.

Wow, what luck! We went straight away to look at it. The farm was in the countryside outside of Anna, about twenty minutes from the university. It was beautiful there, with outcroppings of large boulders, gentle hills, and lush green valleys. There was even a big cave overhang near the property where Indians had lived, probably for thousands of years, and the farm bordered Shawnee National Forest and miles of wilderness.

When we pulled up in our old white Chevy, Hobart and Bess, the brother and sister who owned the place, met us in the drive. They were old-time Southern Illinois country folk. It turned out that the house that was for rent had been their mom's before she passed. It was across the way from their place, far out in the country, with no other buildings in sight.

We took a look at the house. It was a lovely place that stood on top of a hill surrounded by a white picket fence, furnished with beautiful antiques from the 1800s. Such furnishings are a lifelong love of mine. I thought I had died and gone to heaven! The house stood upon a hill overlooking a pond and 1,000 acres of rolling hills with rocks, waterfalls, and lovely pathways, all bordering on forty miles of Shawnee National Forrest. If I could have imagined a place that would fulfill all my dreams, this would have been it. It was uncanny how ideal it was.

Upon talking to Hobart and Bess, we discovered that no one else had even inquired about the farm. In fact, Hobart and Bess—who were somewhat elderly, and simple country folk—barely knew there was a university in Carbondale, much less a housing office. They had not placed the ad. The list had been out for over two weeks, yet no one had called except us. This was very unusual and unexplainable. But it was great! We thanked whatever housing gods were helping us, rented the farm, and drove away mystified.

The next day we got a call from Hobart asking us to please do something to stop all these people from calling about the farm. Apparently, the previous day as we drove away from the farm, their phone began to ring with inquiries and had not stopped ringing since. So, further mystified, we called the housing office and requested on behalf of Hobart and Bess that the listing be withdrawn.

How was it that this farm, which nobody had listed, was on an old campus housing list, and that no one had ever called about it until we rented the place? Hobart and

Bess knew nothing of the university. What had happened was impossible. Yet it occurred. Mystical forces seemed to be in play that were beyond my comprehension. Upon reflection, these forces seemed somehow connected to this farm's being destined to become the setting for a profound mystical opening in both my life and the life of my husband.

The Chicago Trip

We moved into the farm and set a sunny bedroom aside as our meditation room, filling it with plants and an altar. My meditation was going nicely. I enjoyed it, and no unusual experiences were occurring. I was happy.

Some months later, we decided to visit Chicago to see some friends. While there, we decided we wanted to visit a particular esoteric Christian mystic group we had heard about. When we got to Chicago, our friend warned us that this group had a questionable reputation. He said that he had heard that people would go there to visit and never leave. They would remain cloistered for at least six months, not contacting anyone from the outside. When they finally did come out, they would be followers of the sect. Our friend felt that something was not right about this situation and that we should be careful. But we thought we would just go take a look and see what they were like—out of curiosity.

When we got there, we rang the doorbell and asked to enter. We were brought in and advised that their main priest wanted to see us. Upon entering, we both began to experience a strong sensation. We automatically began to say our *mantras* in response. As we walked up the stairs to the office of the head priest, I began to feel a bizarre pressure in my head and body. Things began to look strange, as if I were on a drug. Upon entering the room, we were asked to sit on a couch by the head priest. He sat across from us, and a woman priest sat back a little, silently rocking in her rocking chair. The situation was anything but normal.

Jack and I both continued to repeat our mantras silently, like lifelines. I felt as if tremendous pressure were being applied to my mind. If I could have gotten up and left, I would have, but I could not move. My husband seemed to be in the same predicament. I held my mantra like a shield, realizing I was pitched in a psychic battle and fighting for my survival.

The head priest began speaking to us. He wanted to know who we were. We told him, but the answer did not satisfy him. Already extremely strong, the psychic pressure continued to grow. The room, and our conversation, seemed to undulate in waves. We were novice meditators and quite unprepared for the existence, much less the experience, of this type of psychic battle. At this point, I knew my posture was purely defensive. I was only protecting myself with my mantra, which apparently was working as a psychic shield. Thankfully, it seemed to be reflecting the priests' own psychic force back upon them.

As time went on, there seemed no way out of this situation. I literally could not move. I was barely able to stem the force of the assault, and things were getting pretty strange. I had not thought too much about the Guru, Baba, of whom Dadaji had spoken, but this was really a tight spot. I needed help. The thought of Baba came into my mind. Mentally I called to him with a cry for help. Then suddenly, the two priests lost complete interest in us. At that very instant, the psychic pressure vanished. They said we could go. Things began to look and sound normal again as the pressure lifted, and we quickly left, glad to be out of there.

When Jack and I compared notes afterward, he'd had the same experience as I had, except he had not called out for Baba's help. I shared with him what had happened, and for the first time, I took proper notice of Baba as a guru. I said to Jack, "Wow! I think we may actually have a guru!" It seemed Baba had saved us from becoming two more new disciples of this sect, which clearly had questionable values regarding the use of psychic force and mental manipulation. With this experience, the reality of Baba as my guru first dawned on me.

Many synchronistic mystical occurrences seemed to be happening around this period—first the sudden eviction, then the farm, and now this weird psychic run-in. Then as if this wasn't enough, while we were driving home from this trip to Chicago, I looked up at the sky. The clouds were not simply white. They shimmered with all the colors of the rainbow. I pointed it out to Jack. He saw it also. We stared at the sky in amazement. There seemed to be magic and mysticism all around us.

A strange, transparent disc appeared in the sky a few days after we returned home. The object was seen in five states, but no one could explain what it was. It stayed in the sky for about four days, adding to our sense that things were getting pretty strange. The official government's explanation was that it was a weather balloon, but nobody believed that. We, along with others, thought it was a UFO. It was just another one of the unexplainable phenomena going on around us.

Shortly after that, back at the farm, I read *Autobiography of a Yogi* by Paramahansa Yogananda, a classic tale of Yogananda's life and the saints of India whom he had met on his spiritual journey. Then one night, I had a dream about Harikhan Baba, a great mystic Himalayan yogi mentioned in the book, who was said to have lived for centuries and is known to have appeared to many people. In my dream, he appeared and spoke some words to me. I awoke from the dream burning up with heat. I was drenched in sweat and on fire, although it was the dead of winter, and the heat was off. It could not have been over 40 degrees in the house. Shortly after, my husband also awoke. He, too, was on fire. Burning with heat and covered in sweat, he threw off the covers and sat up next to me, wondering what was going on.

As soon as he fully woke up, I told Jack about my dream about Harikhan Baba. It was still fresh in my mind—the image of Harikhan Baba and a sense of his presence still consuming my thoughts. We sat in bed as we both cooled down from this unusual body heat and wondered, with more than a bit of awe, if this had been a visitation. After several hours this strange mystical heat subsided, but the wonder remained.

A Vision Given

As with all other unexplainable events, I was living on the farm when a vision of the far-reaching future of humanity unfolded within my inner sight. It was a few weeks after we had returned from Chicago, during this time of magical and mystical happenings. I was lying down, resting on top of the covers in my bedroom. It was late afternoon. I was not asleep, only relaxing after a long day when a flow of information seemed to drop into my mind.

An awareness flows into my mind. I begin to understand that humanity is at a critical juncture in evolution. I see that this is the first of these evolutionary junctures which we will cross. Until now, the human species on this planet has been evolving in a primitive way, gaining a sense of individual development. With this evolution of individuality has come the desire to protect and defend for survival, to improve personal status and well-being. This focus of evolution on the improvement of the individual has served us well in this first and longest phase of our evolutionary process.

I perceive in this phase, as it passes before me, that humanity is growing in its mental capacities. From the invention of the wheel to the development of technology, we progress in geometrical leaps toward the ability to instantly turn ideas into realities. As I remember Buckminster Fuller pointing out, it took half a million years for the concept of a wheel to become a reality. The time between ideas and their manifestation has since been closing at a geometrical rate until the development of ideas and their expression is almost instantaneous.

I see this process as reaching a critical mass. As a species, we manifest our ideas; as we do, our world grows smaller and more interdependent. In technology, we have found the power of self-destruction. I see that as technology evolves and communication increases, we become increasingly linked together. Our fate becomes collective rather than individual. As the vision continues, I see we have reached a juncture where the evolutionary emphasis on personal welfare that has served us in the past is fast becoming a poison that will kill us.

At this stage, a jump must be made. Within me, a knowing arises in which the evolution of the whole species must come forward and take dominance over individual development. I see this not only as a natural evolutionary path but also as a critical juncture we must face and move through—or we will destroy ourselves. Personal greed and territorialism must bow to the collective nature of humanity's future. As this vision continues, I realize this is only the first evolutionary juncture.

After this, we enter the second phase. I see humanity blossoming in its collective link through technology and communication systems. Humanity is truly becoming a united species, growing in capacity. As this second phase continues and technology reaches its full development, I see human beings gaining increasing psychic development. Communications begin to take place not only through primitive physical devices but by mental linkage. And again, a critical juncture is reached. This phase takes much less time than the first phase of our evolution.

I now see that at this second juncture, humanity must face its capacity to link mentally. Individuality is thinning. With mental linkage, the evolutionary track again changes. Collective soci-

ety gives way to inter-psychic development. Meanwhile, human physiology is also changing. Cranial structures are developing, and other functions are altering. As mental and psychic capacities develop, individuals become more attuned and blended.

Then I see a third juncture where an actual linking occurs among all members of the species. Like cells in a giant brain or small parts of a collective mental whole, the collective mind forms out of the linked individuals. Evolution jumps from individual entities within the species to emphasis on the development of the collective mind. Each evolutionary juncture comes far faster than the preceding one until the last junctures are almost instantaneous, one following the other. The greatest time spent was by far in the first evolutionary stage.

Another juncture now occurs. Individuals directly linked in a collective species become more subtle. There are several evolutionary junctures I see continuing in this vision. All lead from physical individuals that are psychically linked to the shedding of biological evolution. I see the human species' mental growth as an entity composed of many small, individual minds melded together.

Finally, a juncture unfolds in collective mental development where knowledge becomes instantaneously available. I see this collective mind exploring the far reaches of knowledge, losing its need for primitive physical expression. The human minds are entirely merged and collectively developing beyond the need for physical bodies. At this stage, the physical species passes from existence. Then I see this collective entitative mind taking in knowledge at an almost instantaneous pace, becoming the universe, evolving to pure consciousness, and completing the cycle of creation.

My awareness is brought back to the room around me. Rising from where I had been lying and the vision that had unfolded, I begin to pace the room, wondering if I have, indeed, been shown the far-reaching future of humanity.

Later I learned that somewhat similar ideas were presented in a book called *Childhood's End*. However, I had never heard of this book, much less read it. Nor had I heard of any ideas similar to those that had unfolded in my mind. It was part of the mystery of the mystical unfoldment that was beginning to occur around me and within me.

The Mystery Continues

A few months later, in perhaps February of 1971, as I got up from my meditation, I became aware of an unusual experience. Suddenly, like awakening from sleep and becoming aware of a forgotten dream, I became aware of an experience I had been having during my meditation. Awareness dawned on me that I had been listening to a voice speaking to me during meditation. Suddenly I recalled that not only had I listened to this voice speaking to me during this meditation, but I had heard him each time I had meditated, which I had done twice daily over the last three months. Each time I meditated, this sweet voice would come into my mind, speaking words of love and compassion—and after each meditation, the memory of the experience would fade. I would only recall a peaceful and pleasant meditation.

Now, suddenly, I was recalling these forgotten experiences. The mysterious voice I had heard during my meditations was distinctly male and unbelievably kind. Like a thief in the night, this one had softly come into my mind without my awareness and stolen my heart. Every word he spoke in my mind was a droplet of pure love. He was love personified. Every word charmed me. By the time I recalled this experience, my heart was already taken. He was all I had ever wanted, all that I had ever searched for. He was the personalized form of the Universal Love I thought I had lost. He was the Beloved of my childhood, whom I had forgotten as I grew. He was the manifestation of the divine love, of which all human love is a shadowy reflection. This one came tenderly into my mind, calling himself Baba.

As the memory of my experiences with him reached my conscious mind, I was torn between the love of my heart and the fear in my rational mind. At that time, I had heard of no one hearing voices in their mind except schizophrenic people. I was already very prone to fear, and I felt that I had mental problems. To my rational mind, this confirmed it. Only a crazy person would listen to voices in their mind. Yet I was already in love. He was the bright sun illuminating the darkness. His love was unbearably sweet, his kindness without limit. How could any mere human to whom he revealed himself refuse him?

Even at that time, I realized the kind way he had handled my situation. If he had begun to speak to me, as he had done a year earlier, and allowed me to recall the experience, I would have again become terrified and stopped my meditation. So, he had come to me secretly, keeping the knowledge of his presence from my waking mind. Then, when my heart was already secured, he allowed my mind to have knowledge of him. I have always found this wisdom to be his skill and ability. He is the master craftsman who sculpts human minds with strokes of pure love. My rational mind concluded I had gone off the deep end, listening to an internal voice. Yet I realized that if listening to this sweet Beloved was madness, I would have to be mad.

Thus, I came to know Baba, my true guru, who revealed himself to me in the inner realm. I was still timid and fearful. I did not readily accept the experiences I was having. But when he came near me, all fear would fly from my mind. Each word was a drop of nectar, soothing and healing me. His words formed honey that coated my mind in love. I would be lost in the ecstasy of his divine Presence. He was the solid rock that could hold my being. His love was the safe haven this transitory world could not provide. Only his love was more potent than fear. This guru, this Baba from within, soon became the cornerstone of my life.

The Second Awakening

After all of the magical and mystical events that had begun happening, and now with the revelation of the inner presence of Baba, a time of intense spiritual activity opened in my life. I began to experience Baba as a great ship, a vast spiritual entity that moved very close, overshadowing my small existence. I began to hear his lovely voice, not only in *sadhana*, meditation, but at different times during the day. He became my constant companion. I would lose all interest in worldly life when he would fill my awareness. Enchanted by his loveliness, lost in the bliss of love, I cared nothing for this world.

Then, he would move apart from me, and agony would strike. Old fears and anxiety would swim to the surface in the pain of separateness. Doubt would consume me, and he would fade from reality like a dream. Only the mundane world would appear to be real. Then again, after some time, the waters of my mind would calm, and his image would rise from the depths, strong and solid. He would again take reality in my mind, and my heart would sing. My Beloved would be near. Like this, my mind swung back and forth between two worlds. Half of the time in bliss—and half in fear, doubt, and disbelief.

Then one day, when he first began talking to me, he said, "I am your *Kula Guru*." I did not know Sanskrit and had certainly never heard of this term. I asked him to spell it for me and wrote it down. I thought, "Now, am I making up words, or is this truly some Sanskrit term I do not know the meaning of?" Determined to find out if it was, in fact, a word and what it meant, I went to the university library and got out a large Sanskrit/English dictionary. I looked up the term Kula Guru. In fact, lo and behold, it was indeed a word! But the dictionary said it meant sheepherder. I couldn't get how this related, but I had no other place to look.

It was not until later in India, sitting at the feet of my physical guru, that I would learn the meaning of this important statement regarding his nature. Of course, I didn't know this would happen in the future. The only reference I had was the Sanskrit dictionary. I was happy to know that at least it was a word, not just some crazy rambling of my mind. My internal Baba also told me he was my guru, Shrii Shrii Anandamurti. This didn't seem possible to me. Yet when the reality of him came into focus, I would believe the things he said, my heart open and happy. As he distanced a little, my practical mind would take over, and I could not believe these things. At one point, this inner Baba said to me, "You are not capable of understanding your experiences at this point. You do not have the framework. So do not try to understand; simply accept what is happening to you."

At one point, he encouraged me to go alone to Chicago to visit some spiritual friends. I had been depending on my relationship with my husband since the LSD fear arose, and I did not do things alone. But Baba insisted, so I faced my fears and went. At that stage, I was getting so internally drawn that I was not fully present in external interactions. I tolerated them, but my genuine interest was in my internal Beloved.

I was listening to the voice of divine love. Each word Baba spoke had a purity and intensity of caring that is only mirrored in human love. I had found the moon, not merely its reflection, and could not look away. I would wander by myself, listening to my Baba's sweet conversation, asking him questions, and listening to his explanations. I was learning, yet the point was not learning but being in his ineffable love.

I recall going to a park where again, like when I was a young girl, I could see the structures of the people's minds as they passed by. Part of the time, I still thought I had gone off the deep end. But then he would come close, a presence that was ecstasy. If only the world could see him, all eyes would turn from this mundane existence.

As my heart opened to this sweet inner presence, he pulled me to him and away from the dependent relationship I had developed with my husband. Jack became annoyed with me and started to think I was a bit strange, immersed in this inner love. I realized I was withdrawn from the world and continued to fear. But the sweetness and extreme kindness of Baba enchanted me. Despite my fear and my husband's criticism, I could not turn away.

A day came when my husband announced he was going to Jamaica for a few weeks, due to the chaos my inner directedness was creating between us. School was out. I would be alone at the farm. By this time, I was becoming lost in a constant experience of divine love in the presence of Baba. I could not take my mind off him. He was my beloved, divine Father, the one I had always loved. Now that I had found him, I had no interest in anything else. The world was like tasteless food. It was dim and colorless compared to him.

As I grew more deeply immersed in mystical states, I quickly lost my ability to function in the external world. I entered two weeks of such intense spiritual opening that I lost all capacity to care for myself. On the day my husband left, I recall going to the grocery store at the suggestion of my inner guide. I was already beyond noticing such worldly concerns as food. But this caring guide, knowing the distracted condition of my mind, began to take charge of my physical care. Explaining that I needed to purchase food, he guided me to the store, and then, as my mind was entirely distracted, he had to tell me to pick up specific items to purchase as I went through the aisles.

Having secured food with his assistance, I hitchhiked and walked the 15 miles home to my farm, where I would be alone for two weeks. It is difficult to explain this distracted state of mind I had entered. It is as if my being was overshadowed by his. My mind was lost in longing and the experience of unconditional love; I could not attend to this world or my physical care. Had anyone been around, I don't know what they would have thought. But no one was around to interfere as he took me through this process. Conveniently my husband was gone, all worldly involvements on hold, no one about, and I was on the farm we had so miraculously been given. It was clear to me that this situation was no coincidence. It was his hand.

During this period of seclusion, my Beloved took me through intense mental cleansing. I was lost in the experience. His beautiful cosmic presence would be near, enfolding me in bliss, embodying perfection and absolute love. Like Krishna in the *Bhagavad Gita,* all the world was a shadow next to him. I ached with every particle of my being to forget this dusty earth and merge in him for eternity.

Then again, as had been happening, my mind would cycle away from him, and my being would wrench with agony. He would seem unreal, and again I would see myself as a crazy person, loving someone who did not exist. Doubt would fill me, fear rising to the surface, consume me. When I was pushed to the edge, he would come close again, showering me with ecstasy and love.

In this way, he worked with my mind, creating experiences. He had me go through my entire life, reliving it, reexperiencing it, and writing it all down. I have found that over the years, he has a certain ability to create and recreate experiences, in my mind and other people's. He talks, and then I experience what he says. During this time, my Baba had me go back through my birth from conception onward. With his aid, I vividly experienced the time in my mother's womb, my birth, my mother's close encounter with death, and all the fear and pain of my earliest years, writing it down as he instructed. When I could take no more, he would come close again, enfolding me in divine love. Melting in the shelter of this love, I would heal. He took me through all the pain and fear of my life, recreating in my mind moments of terror.

In the dark of the night, I hear monsters walking about outside. I know this is a tantric test he is creating in my mind, and I know the purpose—to bring out fear, forcing me to face terror and not run from it. For hours on end, this is going on, but he breaks it at just the right time, and my Beloved comes to me, enfolding me in divine Presence. In the depths of this process of love and pain, I give up all hope of sanity. I surrender to the realization that by following this loving guide, I have become hopelessly lost to the world. But I have come to love him more than even my sanity.

My mind is gone in this process; I cannot care for my body. He continues to look after this body with kindness, directing me to eat now with specific instructions as to what food to take. Then lost to this world, I hold the food in my hands. He reminds me to actually eat, and so I follow his instructions. Thus, my guide looks after this body while taking me through this deep inner process.

I am having trouble expressing the extent of this infinite tenderness, care, and compassion. Illumining my being with his effulgence, he took me to him like a babe in its mother's arms, controlling the circumstances in my life and washing away the dirt and pain that had accumulated. This period of seclusion was spent partly in ecstasy and partly in fear and pain. Then, when this time was nearing a close, Baba told me that I should write the story of my birth and my past and burn it. He said, "It is finished. Write it, burn it, and leave it behind." Which I did.

On the last day before my husband Jack was to return, I sat in the sun on a hill behind our house covered with soft green grass. The day was warm, and the scents of earth and leafy things warming in the sun filled the air. The presence of my beloved Baba came wafting into my mind. But this afternoon, he was not gentle; he was stern with me. He became furious with me.

As I sit on the grass, Baba begins to speak. His presence is strong. In a scathing tone, he says, "You have wasted your life in self-criticism and self-pity. You do not deserve my assistance. I have come to help you. Look what I have had to do to get you out of the mess you have made of your life. You don't deserve me. I will leave you now."

His fury stuns me. All my doubts and fears of delusion are gone in the reality of his words. There is nothing to be said in my defense. The thought that he would truly leave me pierces my heart. Humbled, I fall in full pranam, lying with my hand stretched above my head, face down upon the grass; I plead with him with all my heart. In my mind, I say to him, "Baba, please do not leave me, I beg you. Stay with me. Do not leave, I beg you."

There is a moment of mental silence. The power of his mind focuses on me as he gazes in judgment, taking in all that I have ever been or will be. I see, reflected in his mind, my past lives layered one upon the other like a deck of cards. I cannot read them. They move by too quickly for me, but I know he sees them. He judges me not for who or what I am in that moment, but in the totality of my existence.

Then, with the ease of someone turning up the volume on a radio dial, he melts my being into his with increasing intensity. This world dissolves from view, and I become lost in his white effulgence. Every particle of my being melts into his infinite, boundless love beyond words, leaving only the slightest thread of my existence.

This deeply fulfilling union lasts an undefinable time. Slowly the world comes back into view. Baba's love surrounds me. I find I am still lying on the lawn. He says, "Now you should come to India to be with me physically." From this point on, he begins to encourage me to come to his physical presence. But India seems very far from Southern Illinois, and I am a very timid person. Yet I want to go.

Later when I reflected upon my experience, I realized that this profound union with my internal Beloved held not only bliss but an element of discomfort. Within the experience, the thin thread of separation had been a wrenching pain. But I also realize that he had probably given me all he dared, given my body's lack of preparation. Had he come closer, had he severed that thread, perhaps I would have lost this physical structure.

As it was, after that experience, each time I would sit for sadhana or meditation, an excruciating pain would start at the base of my spine. As I continued to say my mantra, the pain would rise up my spine until it spread to my body's upper portions. It would become so intolerable after 15 or 20 minutes of sadhana that I could not continue. I recall having to break my meditation and grab a bed railing, squeezing it to hold on until this pain slowly receded down my spine. Although this process was challenging and I could not tolerate meditation for an extended period, I continued sadhana twice daily on the instruction of my inner Baba. After a month or so, this pain with meditation passed.

The day after my profound experience of Baba, Jack returned home from Jamaica. The trial that Baba had put me through was over. Although I was absorbed in continual thoughts of and conversation with Baba, I could care for my body and function again. With Baba's strong encouragement, I suggested selling everything and going to India. My husband, who himself was not unaffected by Baba, agreed.

We dropped out of school, gave notice on our farm, sold all our furniture and other belongings, and found homes for our dog and two cats. However, we still didn't have enough money to go to India, so we stayed with my parents near Chicago and got jobs to earn the rest of our passage. I worked for about three months as a waitress to save money.

During these three months in Chicago, I began to experience different aspects of Baba. Like the facets of a magnificent jewel, he began to manifest divine qualities. One after the other, those various aspects of his being would unfold before me—each shimmering with an excruciating beauty. For about a week, each word my Baba said in my mind was the absolute expression of perfection. It was as if in all the universe, in the entire configuration of the cosmos, the absolute expression of perfection forms itself into a drop of nectar and is released in a single word spoken by him within my mind. The power of his words stunned me. How can a mere human look upon perfection? It is nearly intolerable.

Then he began to become the expression of absolute justice. In his words, the perfection of justice found manifestation. It was not the reflection we see in human dealings but the essence. The pure source, the unadulterated expression. If in all the world, one word could be said that would embody justice in its absolute form, that one singular expression, that perfect moment, would drop into my mind in a single word spoken. This small mind could barely contain such a sight.

Then he became compassion in its most absolute expression. Again, it stunned my mind. Then he was the very expression of perfect, unbearable beauty. These qualities he revealed to me were the pure aspects that find reflection in human interaction. They were the direct light of his mind in their pure expressions, stunning and almost intolerably exquisite. That which I see in the world about me is only a mirrored reflection.

I was absorbed with him whenever I was not working, or external demands did not pull me away. He was kind to me beyond words. As my constant companion, he soothed my fears, encouraged me to believe in myself, gave me unconditional compassionate love, taught, advised, revealed himself to me, and guided me. He was the bright light in my life. No amount of love could repay the kindness he displayed toward me. In his sweetness, I found actual shelter, my true home.

Chapter V
Travels to India

*B*y May 1971, Jack and I finally had enough money to buy tickets and go to India. We purchased one-way tickets, not knowing if or when we would ever be back. All we knew was that we had to see Baba. We couldn't think beyond that. So, we got our shots and visas, and, to save money, we purchased tickets on a small Arab airline. As it turned out, these were not the best planes.

But before we found that out, we went to New York and stayed with some friends who had just returned from seeing Baba in the town of Ranchi. They told us to go to Patna, the capital of Bihar state, as Baba was moving there.

While staying in their apartment, I noticed a book called *The Life of Ramakrishna*. I picked it up, began looking through it, and could not believe what I was reading! *Ramakrishna* had had experiences much like mine, yet he did not question his sanity. He was a great spiritual man. Reading about his experiences was a profound revelation for me. I realized that other people had experiences like mine.

When reading the *Bhagavad Gita,* I understood that experiences of universal divine love existed outside of

LSD. That they were real. Reading about Ramakrishna, I realized that other sane people experienced a personalized revelation of the sacred. A huge weight was taken from my mind. I took a deep breath and sighed, knowing my experiences were not mad ravings.

While we were in New York, and even back in Chicago, people began to tell us stories about our guru, Shrii Shrii Anandamurti Baba. The stories were amazing, including ones about Baba being seen in two places at the same time, hundreds of miles apart, and speaking over 200 languages. They said he knew everything you were thinking, put people into deep spiritual states with a touch or glance, performed miracles, and could talk about any subject and know things no one else knew. He seemed like a pretty magical guy.

Later I came to hear the stories in more depth and discovered for myself that these things were, in fact, true. I also found out later that Anandamurti Baba was known for some political and humanitarian ideas he was putting forward called PROUT and Neohumanism. Like Aurobindo, he would come to be arrested for his thoughts, and his movement banned while I was in India seeing him. But I did not know any of this at the time.

With excitement to meet Baba in physical form, and light hearts, Jack and I boarded a plane from New York to England. I had never been on a plane or traveled outside the country. So, when I got on the plane, fear loomed inside of me, even though it was a modern jumbo jet. My inner guide, kind as always, stood by me with soft words and gentle encouragements, quelling my fears. His presence made the intolerable tolerable.

When we got to England and changed planes, boarding the Arab airline we had bought tickets on, we had a disquieting surprise. It was an old American jet that had been retired from use and then been purchased second-hand. It was outdated and only three seats wide. No one spoke English. The plane could only hop from one country to another, so we saw Eastern Europe and the Arab world country by country and were often met at the airports by armed guards.

At one point after takeoff from Damascus (Syria), the stewardess began announcing something important and serious by her tone of voice. Everyone took on a concerned demeanor. A Jesuit priest sitting next to us pulled out his rosary and began saying prayers. It could not be good. Jack and I gave each other worried glances and looked out the window to discover that the engine was smoking. Something was clearly wrong, but no one spoke English. Finally, the priest spoke enough English to tell us the engine was failing, and we would have to force land. My husband and I just thought of our guru, Baba; we meditated, and waited, watching as we passed low over mud huts sunken into the ground. Finally, the pilot landed the plane successfully at a small airport in Kuwait, where guards holding bayonets lined both sides of a walkway while we were herded into a waiting room. We spent some nervous hours under guard before we were allowed to leave aboard another plane and continue our journey. After several more days, this sketchy trip ended when we landed in Delhi.

What a shock when we finally got off the plane! There were beggars everywhere, crippled children with hands held out asking for food, a man with no legs in a wagon crying out for alms, crowds of people, and chaos. Honking horns, rickshaw bells, men carrying platters of tea, yelling "Chai, Chai" in gravelly voices, and smells of Indian spices and cookfire smoke combined in a din of confusion.

Then suddenly, our names were being called over a loudspeaker. I couldn't believe it. We were found by a man sent to meet us, who escorted us to a private room where a devotee of our guru, who held an important government post, met us and, much to our relief, invited us to stay at his house. We were escorted around customs and into a private car. I felt so grateful and cared for, as if by Baba's hand.

Soon we were comfortably at this man's home, meeting various devotees of our guru and hearing many stories about Baba. I could not wait to meet this physical Baba! We were given time to rest and adjust to the time change and the culture. It was a shock being there, yet somehow, something about India was more comfortable, making me feel more at home than in the country of my birth.

After a few weeks in Delhi, we boarded a train for Patna, the capital of Bihar state, to see Anandamurti Baba. We decided to save money and travel third class. Little did we know what we had signed up for. When we got on the train, we had to push through a crowd of passengers, wall to wall inside the car, until we got to a bench someone kindly offered us. Sitting on a crowded three-tier platform, amid a mass of people shoved one against another—some even hanging off the back of the train—we huddled together. We sat amid legs dangling from the platform above ours, the earthy smells of so many people packed together, and the din of voices and screechy train sounds for some twenty hours as we crossed India.

When we finally reached Patna, a small, dirty city with mud streets, we went from the train to the *ashram* on the only available transport, a rickshaw. A greasy-looking Indian man with no English and bad teeth, dressed in dirty whites, smiled at us from his rickshaw, a bike with a wide seat behind it for passengers, as we tried to explain where we were going. Unsure if he really understood, we set out, hopefully for the ashram. We passed three-sided shacks selling food, town buildings with bright-colored signs in Hindi, and rice paddies with trees and walkways between. Amid the smell of Indian spices and cookfires, we pushed past buffalo wandering the streets, ox carts, men haggling in open markets, and a rare car.

I thought I heard *Baba Nam Kevalam*, a chant to Baba, continually playing in the distance. I told Jack, "People here must all be very devoted," but I could not see anyone chanting and, after some time, began to realize that this was not exactly an external sound. Somehow the sounds of India were becoming a song for me that was dedicated to Baba.

When our rickshaw driver pedaled up to the ashram where we would be staying, we were met by a rag-tag group of Westerners and some Indian gentlemen wearing *lungis* and *kurtas*, the traditional Indian dress for men. The building was a large cement structure, much like those around it. Across the street, women dressed in dirty *saris* carried full baskets on their heads as they walked barefoot across rice paddies. The air smelled of incense and moist dirt. We went inside to settle in.

We were in the backwaters of India, and it was 1971. The culture was traditional, with little disturbance by Western technology. There were no TVs, no radios, and no refrigerators. Women stayed in their homes unless accompanied by a male relative and wore their saris with the ends thrown up, veiling their heads, eyes down in the presence of men. The men we met were college educated and spoke English, but their wives and sisters were uneducated and illiterate. We could not talk to them. Sometimes I felt the cows had more status than the women. I was something out of place there, not a woman by their standards of behavior and not a man. Yet they seemed to accept me and be fascinated by our Western ways.

The ashram was filled with young people like us from Europe and America. We were given a room in the ashram, where we slept on a concrete floor in our cotton sleeping bags. Oh yes, and there was no furniture in the ashram. They called it a *Jagreti*, and we were in the real India of that time. People sat on the floor. And we had come not to visit, but to live.

Meeting Shrii Shrii Anandamurti

I was nervous to see Baba as a physical guru. After all, what is the relationship between this external person and my internal Baba? This question of the relationship between them was foremost for me. I wanted to ask my physical guru if he was the same as my inner guru. My internal Baba always insisted they were the same, but that did not seem rational. Who was this I was going to meet? I had heard great stories, and I was confident he did know everything about each of us, could speak any language, and performed miracles, as everyone had said. But who was he really? Did I already know him, or was he someone different? I had come on the urgings of my internal Beloved; now, I did not know what I would find.

The very first day we were at the ashram, after settling in our room, we were invited to come for evening darshan. Darshan, a Sanskrit word, means "site of the guru," or seeing him whenever he shows up to give a talk. This was what we had come for! So, when it was time, smiling and brimming with excitement, hardly noticing the twenty feet from our room on the other side of a small courtyard, we floated over for his talk. Still hippies, I came wearing my bell bottom pants, my long, auburn hair flowing, and Jack had donned a clean white kurta over his jeans. We were going to see our guru!

Sunshine on our faces, we entered the darshan room. It was an L-shaped room with people sitting on the floor, primarily Indian men and a few women to the side. A kind of platform bed with pillows stood at the front of the hall, I assumed for Baba. There was a door to the right through which Baba would come in.

As we entered the room, a guard in a gray uniform immediately met us, informing us that Jack would have to sit with the gentlemen, and I with the ladies. We didn't expect this. Much to my surprise, I was escorted to a small side section and told that only men could sit in front of Baba. Because I was a woman, I had to sit to the side with the ladies. I was also told that I was not allowed to dance *kirtan*, a traditional *bhakti* yoga practice that involves dancing while chanting sacred names. My smile was gone, and my face flushed. Ruffled, I sat down as instructed, but I was disturbed. My Baba had not warned me about these things.

Soon Anandamurti Baba entered the room. My eyes focused on him; my excitement returned. I had traveled halfway around the world for this moment! He was walking in, dressed in white Indian attire with black shoes and no socks. His hands folded in a prayer position, he greeted us as he entered. I noticed he was short, probably a little over five feet, with golden skin, short hair, a handsome face, and black-rimmed glasses. A classic family man of the times, he was trailed by orange-robed monks who took seats near him. Baba then sat on the platform bed facing the men in the front of the room.

As he began to give his talk, instead of the bliss I expected or knowledge that he was my Baba, I found that, much to my embarrassment, every thought I would never want to think in front of an all-knowing being who could read my mind, was pulled to the surface. I spent my first weeks near my physical guru, attempting uselessly to control my thoughts. Finally, when I realized it was hopeless and gave up, the process stopped.

As this purging process began to settle, an increasing awareness of precious energy around Baba started to arise. A growing connection to this external Baba began to form in my mind as I began to feel the blissful flow of his energy. I became enchanted by his smile, the way he gestured with his hands, the way he reclined like Lord *Krishna*, and the compelling sound of his voice, like the Cheshire cat. He mesmerized me. Listening to his talks, gazing up at him, I saw Krishna charming the *Gopis*, and then again other times, he was *Shiva*, immovable like a mountain—the great Lord of all creation.

I settled into the pattern of morning and evening darshans with this mystical guru and began to find his vibration the same as what I felt when my inner Baba would talk to me. Though he was a separate person and a great spiritual master—and as such, I was quite intimidated by him—there was a vibrational similarity to my internal guru that was unmistakable. After some time, my love and attachment to my physical guru began to match the love I felt for my Baba's inner form. I felt as magnetically pulled to him as to my inner Baba, perhaps even more. Each was extremely lovable, for me, the nearest and dearest and kindest of beings.

Chapter VI
My Time with Baba

Once I had settled into the ashram, my days began to consist of meditating, seeing Baba in darshans mid-morning and before dinner, taking a few classes here and there from the monks on everything from following a *sattvic* diet to cosmology, and meeting periodically with my *Acharya*, the one who gave me my meditative practices and guided me personally.

My Acharya, or teacher, was a family man who lived just a few blocks from the ashram and was a personal friend of Anandamurti Baba. He was a delightful older man, with warm eyes and a generous smile, named Kadarjii. This humble Indian man exuded the spiritual grace and wisdom I sought. I was very fond of him, and he taught me well. He would periodically invite Jack and me over for dinner, getting us out of the ashram. His wife would cook delicious Indian food, and when we dined with them and their daughters, they were always gracious. Though the women spoke no English, they managed to communicate in their own way. This was a part of the simple India of those days that I came to love.

The room where Jack and I stayed in the ashram was small and a bit barren. We had a small altar against one wall and our cotton sleeping bags in the center of the room on the bare concrete floor. These simple cotton sleeping bags were our only comfort furnishings. Our door opened out into a small courtyard. In this room, I did my long hours of meditation, except when I would sit and meditate for several hours in the darshan hall before Anandamurti Baba's talks. The sleeping bags served as sleeping mats, meditation cushions, and a mat for my daily *asanas* or yoga postures.

When not meditating or in darshan, we would visit with the other residents or go out to the Indian Bazaar and shops to buy food or other items. It was always an interesting experience, as nothing could be purchased without haggling for the price. I got quite good at it.

However, as I have said, most of my time was devoted to long hours of meditation and seeing Baba, either in the twice-a-day darshans or in subtle form alone in my room while in a meditative state of mind. Baba's guidance, both as an external guru and as an internal guide, was my life. I had finally found the Beloved of my heart, the embodiment of a divine being. I had no plans to leave, ever, and would not have if circumstances had not eventually made it necessary. I was with my guru, and that was amazing.

I found that although Anandamurti Baba's darshans appeared to be universal teachings for everyone, he would often start speaking to my questions, concerns, or thoughts. I observed that other people also had this experience. Though his talks were for everyone on the surface, I realized there were specific teachings for certain people in the room.

One darshan that has remained with me over the years occurred about a month into my stay in India. As I mentioned earlier, when my inner guru first came to me, he told me he was my *Kula Guru*, but I could not find any meaning of the term in the Sanskrit/English dictionary at the college, except sheep herder. In this darshan, Baba spoke of the term Kula Guru, and I felt he was talking directly to me, answering my long-held questions. He began by explaining that Kula Guru is a *tantric* term and proceeded to devote the entire darshan to elaborating on it. He noted that in tantra, the Kula Guru is the one who guides the *kula kundalini* from the base of the spine at *Muladhara chakra* to the top of the head at *Sahasvara chakra* and unlocks the union of the little self with the great. It was also noted that the family guru is often referred to as your Kula Guru.

Stunned and absorbed in his explanations, I was deeply touched. No one knew of my experience back in Southern Illinois or the significance of this term to me except Baba. My heart opened, and I felt reassured about the validity of my experiences and Baba's presence. This word he had given me was an accurate word of significance. Baba really *was* my Kula Guru. The darshan was given with simple charm, in the discreet and sweet manner I have come to know as his way. Afterward, I felt deeply grateful to him for taking the time to explain what he had told me internally.

Shrii Shrii Anandamurtijii Baba

Feeling Ignored

As we stayed in India, my internal experience with Baba continued to be blissful, and in his covert way, he was very attentive. However, my external experience of being near him was filled with struggles because I was a woman. As I have mentioned, it began with the first darshan when I was told I would need to sit to the side. I was not allowed to sit in front of Baba. The L-shaped room used for darshan had the flat wooden platform Baba sat on, facing the long section where the men sat. The ladies' section was to his left side.

Baba would come in and sit facing forward, addressing the men and ignoring the women except for an occasional glance. Everyone seemed quite all right with the arrangement, the Indian women quite content, but I was miserable. I felt ignored, and the more I became attracted to this external Baba, the more intolerable the situation became. To add insult to injury, I discovered that Baba would not see women for personal contact. I was told that men could go for a field walk with Baba and have private sessions, where they had profound experiences, but that women were barred from this personal communication with guru. He would not see me.

I could not believe it, and I could not accept it! Various men would tell me and other women their amazing spiritual experiences in this personal contact with Baba. I loved their stories and was happy for them, but each tale wounded me. How could my guru deny me? I had come all the way to India to see him, and I wanted to ask my burning question about the inner and outer guru. On the inner plane, Baba had stolen my heart. How could he bar me from his physical presence?

I would sit in darshan, seeing Baba from the side while he spoke and laughed with the men. I felt completely ignored by him—and miserable. I couldn't stand it. I could not take this rejection. I could not believe for one minute that this was an accident, that it just happened to be how he treated women, and that I just happened to be a woman in this life. I knew with certainty it was more than that. I knew I was close to him. I knew it, but he would not acknowledge me. He ignored me on the pretense of my being a woman.

If this was the problem, why was I not a man? Or why did I not see him in a different setting? The relationship between guru and disciple is profound, and I felt internally committed. I took rejection quite personally. He was the one I had loved life-long, the one I had searched for and cried for, and now that I had found him in form, he would not see me! He would not even look at me in darshan. After this went on for a while, he went so far as to begin skipping me when giving *namaskar* to everyone before he left. A gesture with hands in a prayer position, he would turn first to the ladies, giving his blessing before leaving. However, when he faced where I was sitting, he would lift his hands up and then down so as to ignore me!

I would leave those early darshans, my mind in turmoil and my spirit restless. In subtle form as guru, he would be there. He would hold me while I cried bitterly. He would comfort me with soothing words and gentle love. He would also encourage my rebellion.

I knew Anandamurti Baba was skipping me in giving his blessing in darshan because I was not acting on the guidance of my inner Baba to stand up and do something about the situation. Yet I felt timid and afraid to make waves. However, the problem soon grew intolerable for me. I began to complain and argue with people about the attitudes towards women. Many Western men and women shared my feelings. Even some Indian *Acharyas*, monks and nuns, were sympathetic, but the central office defended their traditional policies.

Women's Rights

It was not long before, at my inner Baba's encouragement, that I decided, along with a group of Westerners, to take the situation in hand. We asked for a meeting with the central office of the monks to push for change. The morning before that meeting, Baba gave darshan and began speaking about the various injustices done to different groups of people. He talked about injustices of castes, race, and other groups, describing how downtrodden people must fight for their rights in the face of injustice. He went on to comment that each group had won their rights through their efforts and struggle and that rights were not simply given. They had to be won. Of course, he did not mention women. He spoke of various causes, but what he was saying to us covertly was very clear-cut.

As a group, we—the Westerners—felt wholly supported. However, what was amazing was that the very monks we would confront later that day seemed to hear none of this in the darshan. It was as if it went right over their heads. When we did meet with the monks in charge, they would not budge from their position about women. They were Indian men, and this treatment of women was all they knew.

Soon after, in protest, we decided that if women could not sit before Baba, the Western men and women would sit to the side. So, on that day before darshan, most of us Westerners, about ten or eleven men and women, sat together in the ladies' section to the side. Baba came and gave darshan in this awkward situation, with us sitting behind the Indian ladies. Then when the kirtan chant started, towards the end of darshan, we all rebelliously stood up, both men and women, behind the Indian ladies and began dancing.

Baba was facing the men's section when he swung around toward us in a smooth motion. As he moved, a piercing, ecstatic wave emanated from him towards us. Since I was in the front, it hit me first. The next thing I knew, I was on the floor doing pranam, kneeling, and I bowed down in surrender. As this wave passed through our ranks, the others also fell to the floor in prostration before Baba. It was an ecstatic revelation of the *Shakti*, spiritual energy, of Guru. We were literally swept off our feet, and left humbled and surrendered before the cosmic wave from him.

We remained in this position as Baba left the darshan hall. We all enjoyed the bliss of this cosmic touch from Baba but were confused by it. After all, he had stopped us from doing the kirtan dance while chanting. Later we came together to try to understand its meaning. We were all clear that he had, in no uncertain terms, stopped us cold in what we were doing. Therefore, we could only assume he did not entirely approve. There needed to be some error in what we were doing. Yet he had stopped us with a very personal blessing. We did not fully under-stand—but we would not do this tactic again.

After a few days, my inner Baba explained to me that the source of physical Baba's objection was that we were disturbing the Indian ladies, most of whom were simple, illiterate people. They were genuinely disturbed by having the men invade their place. It was a disservice to them. I could feel in Baba's presence his deep love for them and his protection of them from our insensitivity. Yet simultaneously, he rewarded us for our courage in fighting for our rights, and I felt internally that he was still supporting the effort.

We Westerners lived in the ashram. The darshan hall was our living room when Baba wasn't there. It was my habit to go an hour or two before darshans and sit in front of the platform Baba sat on and do sadhana, meditation, until darshan. As the Indian men came in for the program, they would ask me to move to the women's section on the side.

One day, shortly after the incident, another woman and I were meditating in front of Baba's platform before darshan. When the men came and asked me to move, as they usually did, Baba internally told me to stay, not to move. So, I just continued to meditate, not moving. The other sister also remained. However, as the time for darshan grew near, the men began to exert severe pressure, and the other woman finally moved. But I could not, as Baba was telling me in my meditation, "Do not move."

A group of men surrounded me, insisting that I move. It was clear to them that I was being unreasonable and out of place. But I remained, eyes closed in meditation, my mind fixed on Baba, who calmly supported me. A guard became furious in the end when I would not move. He began to threaten me with a big stick that he raised over his head to strike me. Baba said again within my mind, "Don't move." I held to my Baba in meditation, unmoving, and the other men grabbed this guard to prevent him from injuring me.

Then, suddenly, Anandamurti Baba was entering the room. All the men around me had to scramble for their seats. I remained sitting directly in front of Baba, barely a foot from where he would sit, with my internal Baba still telling me not to move.

As Baba Anandamurti came into the room and sat down inches from where I was sitting, an overpowering experience of his love and care for me consumed me. I was lost in waves of bliss, clearly understanding that he approved of my actions. I knew it was his will that I follow the inner guidance as he showered me with his love and blessing. My mind, stunned with light and bliss, could not attend to his words. His presence was too strong.

The next day the central office monks announced that the first two rows on the left side in front of Baba would be reserved for Western women. I had won my place with his inner guidance and grace. Western women soon began to stand and do kirtan before Baba. From my inner Baba, I again felt encouragement and support. From the outer person of Anandamurti Baba, I felt love and blessing. He no longer ignored me in darshans; I had followed his internal guidance. It was clear that he approved, although some of his monks did not seem to.

Thus, Baba taught us to fight for our rights and those of others in need. He taught me to follow his inner guidance, even in the face of danger. He also showed me he would take care of the outer circumstances if I held firm to him. Lessons I would need as my fate unfolded later in life.

Darshans

When I started following Baba's inner guidance about women's rights and acting on it, Baba began to pay attention to me subtly, the wave of his loving presence engulfing me when he entered the room. Immersed in his spiritual presence, I often found it challenging to follow his words, though he spoke in English in those days. His voice was like a golden thread weaving sweetness and love. To be near him was to be home.

I now had my place in front of Baba, as I had desired. I often sat less than a foot from him, feeling like he spoke to others while I was there, close, only to be in the blessing of his presence, which I would be lost in, bliss stunning my mind.

I recall one darshan where Baba sat with a stick. After a time, he began to shout at people and raise his stick. Lost in his presence, my mind could not focus. I was close in front. He reached over my head with his arm, stick in hand, speaking to others. There was no need for me to bother to follow his words. They were for others. I was there to be close to him.

Many days, sitting directly in front of him, I would watch as he slipped off his shoes, inches in front of me, before he brought his legs up to sit cross-legged to give his darshan. Then after talking, when he was to leave, he again put his feet down into his shoes, struggling a bit to get them to slip on before going. Time and again, I watched, wanting to reach out and touch his feet, only inches away, and to assist him with his shoes. I longed with everything in me to touch him. But it was India, and I was a woman, and I would not offend the culture of my guru. So, I held this tension and restraint day after day, month after month. I never experienced Baba's physical touch. My relationship with him was strictly spiritual.

However, I did receive his spiritual touch one day as he gave darshan and demonstrated different states of consciousness, putting one male devotee into various forms of *samadhi*, or spiritual trance. During this time, Anandamurti Baba gave a series of darshans where he would put certain men into different states and have them explain their experience afterward to the people in the darshan hall. He brought one man into the far reaches of space, but mainly he demonstrated different levels of samadhi or spiritual bliss. During this darshan, he was raising the kundalini of a devotee, explaining what was happening as he did so.

Then, as he talked, he glanced at me, catching my eyes. When I met his eyes, they were not ordinary but large and otherworldly, brimming with *Shakti* or divine energy. I was engulfed by his gaze, a powerhouse of spiritual force. Then Shakti shot from his eyes into me. I was stunned. My mind became immobilized by bliss, unable to think. Baba continued with his demonstration for the rest of the people, but I was gone, touched by his glance. Then as Baba left the room, I could not continue to sit up as the bliss was too strong. I fell over in an ecstatic state, where I lay for several hours until my mind slowly began to function again and return somewhat to this world.

As noted, it was my habit during the eight or nine months I was in India seeing Baba to spend most of my day meditating. My meditations were deep and blissful, and I felt Guru's presence always with me. During my time near Anandamurti Baba, he held several large gatherings, called DMCs, around India, each with maybe 70,000 or more people attending, but I did not go. I never saw him give his *mudra* at these large gatherings that people spoke about. But it was by choice that I did not attend. I could not bear to see him surrounded by so many people and for me to be a mere face in a vast crowd. Somehow it was too impersonal, too distant. It did not fit with my sentiment.

Instead, my husband Jack and I would stay behind and care for the ashram. We were ashram managers. I would meditate in front of the dais, or platform bed, on which Baba would sit to give his talks. Each time Baba left, I found that the fabric in the spot where he would sit for darshan would maintain the beautiful scent that always emanated from him. Although I was denied personal contact as a woman, as ashram managers, my husband and I would care for and clean the darshan hall and Baba's personal contact room, where he saw people individually.

When I would go into his private room to clean, the energy would be so high—it was like walking in slow motion through a thick liquid. It was unlike any place I had ever been. The intensity of the vibration in the room was like being on a psychedelic; things were almost undulating, thick with cosmic energy. There was an ecstatic feeling. It was hard to work in that room; I just wanted to sit and go into bliss.

In the darshan hall, there was a rug that people sat on in front of Baba. Each day when I cleaned, I would carefully adjust it closer to his platform so that we could sit closer to Baba. Until one day it became ridiculous, and Baba had trouble getting through. At that point, the monks gave my husband a long lecture. The rug went back out. But after a short time, it somehow slowly inched forward again.

Baba Anandamurtijii
(The Image of Bliss)

Answer to My Questions

For months I sat at Baba's feet, completely in love with this most beautiful entity. It was exceedingly blissful to be near him, but I still yearned to ask Anandamurti Baba about my inner Baba. Were they the same? Due to the customs of the times, he would not see me or talk to me personally, so I could not ask directly. Yet Baba got around this in his subtle way, giving me the answer I needed.

As was his way, he very charmingly and discreetly answered my thoughts regarding this question one day while giving darshan. I was sitting back about four people from Baba when he began speaking about "whom to follow," a theme he had talked about multiple times. He advised "not to follow intellectuals, as they would spout one idea and then another. Not to follow scriptures; some say turn east, some say turn west." Instead, Baba admonished us to "follow the practical man, the yogi."

When he said this, deeply absorbed, looking down at the floor, a thought formed in my mind with an intensity that is clear to this day. I thought, "Baba will not always be before me to physically guide my every step. Whom to follow when he is not physically here? Baba says to follow the practical man, the yogi. My inner Baba is my practical experience of him. When he is not physically before me to guide my every step, I should follow this practical form of Baba that I know, his subtle manifestation as my internal Baba."

As this thought subsided, I suddenly awoke to the fact that I was sitting in darshan, and the room was hushed, totally quiet. Baba had stopped talking. I had been looking down at the floor, lost in these thoughts. Now I looked up, and as I raised my eyes, I met Baba's gaze. He was staring at me. I realized he had stopped speaking and had been looking at me this whole time! It dawned on me that the thoughts I had just been having were from him. As he held my eyes, he nodded yes to this thought! Yes! He was instructing me to follow this inner Baba! I flushed with embarrassment from his attention, broke eye contact, and looked down. He turned and again began to talk, continuing with his darshan. And I knew, beyond a doubt, that he had just given me the answer I was seeking.

A Side Trip to Varanasi

When Baba was gone from the ashram for a few weeks, Jack and I and two friends from the ashram, Dhruva Hobby and Ryan, decided to take a trip to Banaras, or Varanasi as it was called in India, to see the burning ghats. We had heard about Banaras and the burning ghats before we went to India and wanted to see them. So, excited to see more of India, we booked passage on a dusty, worn-looking Indian bus, crowded with people. Even the top of the bus was piled high with luggage and people hanging on, desperate for a ride. We settled in as best we could and endured the long, bumpy passage to Varanasi.

Getting to the city, we secured decent hotel rooms, with running water no less, even though it was cold. The following day Dhruva and Ryan decided to go out early by themselves to explore, and so they were gone when Jack and I got up and set off for the burning ghats. As we approached the old city, we found a maze of narrow streets, about four to five feet wide, with brick walls several stories high on both sides. The buildings were ancient, some of the bricks worn or moss-covered, and holes in these old walls housed little shops with brightly colored silks, rugs, and exotic items for sale.

As we entered the old city, we were soon lost in this maze of narrow, twisty streets. Fortunately, a young boy approached us, saying in pidgin English, "You want to go burning Ghats? I take, for small charge only—few rupees. Need guide? I am guide! For whole day!" Jack and I looked at each other and nodded in agreement. This seemed like a pretty good idea, given that we were already lost. We needed a guide. Jack said, "Yes, yes," to the young man. "Burning Ghats, okay?" The boy nodded, agreeing, "*Thik hai, thik hai*, yes, yes," and headed down the street.

As we meandered through the old city following our guide toward the ghats, where little shops abounded, men called out for us to come in and look at the beautiful rugs, silks, or spices arrayed in their small shops. We stopped and climbed into one to sit on a plush Oriental carpet and view the beautiful silks. The owner, in his grayed whites and a burgundy vest, insisted we take some tea, but the boy whispered for our ears only, "No, no. You will be drugged!" With this warning, shaking our heads "no, no," and motioning, we repeatedly refused the tea until the man finally listened.

With an edge of fear and caution, we soon moved on from this shop. After several such stops in what we knew were somewhat sketchy situations, our guide finally got us to the Burning Ghats. Stepping out of the narrow streets into the open air and bricked paved banks of the Ganges River, the pungent smell of smoke from burning bodies hit us. We saw small boats docked against the brick bank with funeral pyres on them. In another area on the bank, pyres were burning, and people gathered around, crying and lamenting. Hit by smoke, burning bodies, and loud chaos, it was as if we were in another world.

After some time in these burning ghats on the banks of the Ganges, exhausted and overwhelmed, the day growing late, we motioned for our guide to lead us out. Thankful to be out of there and in one piece, we returned to our hotel room by early evening, but our friends were still gone. We became concerned as night came, and they were still not back.

A few hours later, Dhruva and Ryan finally arrived at the hotel and came to our room. Ryan was limping badly, and they both looked a bit shaken. Jack said, "Hey, what happened to you guys? We were starting to get worried." Ryan lumbered in, clearly exhausted, and slumped onto the bed as Dhruva said in a somewhat numb tone, "We got attacked, and I lost my bamboo flute." I commented, "How could you lose your flute? You never part with that thing."

Dhruva sighed and slumped. We pulled over a chair for him. He wearily sat down and then proceeded to tell the most harrowing and amazing story. Apparently, like us, they had made their way down to the Burning Ghats, but without a guide, and had gotten lost in the maze of streets on the way back. They ended up in some back area without people around when suddenly two *Goondas*, or Cutthroats, appeared in front of them with foot-long *Gurkha* knives, with their long, curved blades drawn and ready to use.

They looked around. There was nowhere to run. Dhruva clutched his sacred flute to his chest and thought of Baba—then the bandits attacked, one going after Dhruva and the other Ryan. Dhruva said that he saw the knife and felt it swing across his waist as the bandit pinned him to the wall. He commented that it "felt like something cutting through paper." At this point, Ryan looked up from where he slouched on the bed and said, "As I was fighting off the other guy, I saw the Goonda cut Dhruva across the waist. I was sure he was going to die. The man I was struggling with stabbed me in the thigh. It didn't look good for us."

Then something mind-blowing happened. Ryan glanced up and saw Dhruva's flute blow up in a bright flash of white light, throwing the bandit off of Dhruva onto the ground. The Goonda, who was sprawled on the pavement, looked at his friend, who had stopped attacking Ryan. Both thieves were wide-eyed and stunned. Terrified, they grabbed each other and ran off as fast as possible.

Ryan's leg was injured in the fight, but although they both saw him knifed across the middle, Dhruva did not have a mark on him. His treasured flute was in burnt pieces, scattered across the alley, but he was alive. They both were. With a bit of awe and gratitude for divine grace, they made their way back to the hotel and to us. Ryan spent a few months on crutches, but other than that, all was well. It could have gone very differently without a bit of Baba's cosmic grace and an exploding flute.

Shrii Shrii Anandamurti Baba
The Miracle Worker

Another Miracle

At the ashram, it was perhaps late June or early July when political problems began to break out, and the authorities wanted to arrest Baba. Much like Shri Aurobindo, Anandamurti Baba had stood up for his humanitarian philosophies and was against the popular rule of communism, leaving him unpopular with the powers that be. He left for the hospital to avoid arrest the day before the police came for him, searching the ashram. We had to run out in the rice paddies and hide so they would not take our visas, but after that, life went back to normal—except Baba was not there.

A few weeks passed, and we heard that Anandamurti Baba would be returning. Since we all thought Baba would be gone indefinitely, most people had left the ashram for various points in India. Only a small group of us remained, but we decided to do a 24-hour kirtan, chanting divine names and dancing the traditional kirtan dance brought forward by Chaitanya Prabhu when the Bhakti movement started in the Middle Ages. We did it to welcome Baba back when he got out the next day.

It was a sunny morning when we began the singing and dancing kirtan on the porch of the ashram, thinking it would be just a small group of us. Soon, however, a most unusual phenomenon began to occur. People began returning. First, some people came from south India who just happened to decide to return that day, not knowing Baba was coming back. Then others returned from Bangladesh, where they had been doing relief work. When we inquired as to why, they casually explained that their work had happened to end, so they decided to return.

As we continued with the kirtan, one person after another would show up in a rickshaw, and we would all begin laughing, knowing full well the impossible odds of what was happening. In this way, person after person independently showed up within a few hours. Each person would tell a similar story: nothing special or miraculous had happened to them. They did not know Baba was coming back to the ashram. Circumstances just happened to work out, so it was a good time for them to return.

All but two people from the ashram returned before Baba came for darshan. It was miraculous. So many people in different situations could not turn up at the same time by coincidence. Yet in Baba's typical discreet way, each person's situation was completely natural. There were no psychic messages or profound revelations, just natural circumstances.

I began to feel Baba's immense capacity, as if the universe had moved with him in a natural flow to make the impossible possible. Rather than a psychic power being used, circumstances had naturally configured an outcome that was beyond any odds of coincidence.

In a darshan shortly afterward, when Baba finished talking and was about to leave the hall, I had an opportunity to directly experience his caring intervention and his constant awareness of us all. The men stood to do the kirtan dance while they chanted as usual. As was my habit, I stood along with the men. Baba had never objected to this. But this time, I had not been well for days. I was fragile, yet I stood for Kirtan regardless.

Baba got up to leave as usual. Putting his shoes on, he walked halfway to the door and then suddenly stopped.

He turned around, walked back to his seat on the platform bed, and sat down again, motioning us all to sit. Everyone seemed a bit confused by this break in his usual routine, but we sat down, continuing to sing kirtan, yet no longer dancing. I was relieved by this, as I was too weak to stand. Baba continued to sit for three or four minutes until he was sure no one would get up again. Then he got up and began to leave. As soon as he crossed the threshold, leaving the room, an intense, violent pain started in my abdomen. I became very ill.

I had not realized how ill I was, but Anandamurti Baba had known and, with his usual discreet kindness, helped without calling attention to me. He had stopped me from doing an activity I should not have been doing in my condition and taken my pain from me until he left the room, not to embarrass me in darshan. This was like Baba, as I knew him, both in his subtle and physical forms. This subtlety is part of his charm.

Seeing India

While living at the ashram, Jack and I made some side trips around India, mainly to Buddhist sites. On one of those outings, during the rainy season, we took a car ride to a hill station in the foothills of the Himalayas to a town called Sarnath. It was renowned as the first place that the Buddha taught the *Dharma*. An Indian friend had secured the car for our trip, but the entire state of Bihar was underwater, and we weren't sure we could get through. As we traveled, looking out the window, I saw mile after mile of vast, water-covered lands. Only the roadway was above water. I did not know how these simple people could survive such a flood.

We were finally above the floodwaters when we reached Sarnath, a hill station. There was a nice hotel to stay in and temples with Buddhist artifacts in abundance. The cool mountain air held a feeling of peace. An excellent place for meditation, it provided a beautiful outing.

Yet more significant was our stay in Bodhgaya, just south of Sarnath, where Buddha had sat under the *bodhi* tree and achieved enlightenment. When we arrived in Bodhgaya, we had no place to stay. Yet at that time, there were many Tibetan refugees, and one kind family offered to house us in their tent. The tent was about thirty feet across, with benches surrounding the inside, covered in Tibetan rugs. It was on these beautiful rug-covered benches that we were to sleep. The whole family lived in this tent, working, resting, and sleeping in the same space. The family spoke almost no English but offered us a place to sleep and the food they cooked on an open fire pit outside the tent. The place smelled of Tibetan cooking and incense. Prayer wheels were everywhere and religiously used.

Bodhgaya was a small town back then with various temples, tents, small open-front shops, dirt streets, and a place where the sacred bodhi tree was supposed to be. The first day we were there, we went over to a Tibetan temple that appeared to be newly built and sat in an out-of-the-way side area inside the temple to meditate. A Tibetan monk was painting a section of elaborately painted walls resembling a *thangka* with various deities and demons. Incense wafted through the temple.

After a few hours of meditation, I heard the monks in that deep rumble of Tibetan chanting. I opened my eyes with difficulty, as I was deep in meditation, and saw them sitting facing each other in two lines that ran down from the main altar, chanting, ringing bells or cymbals. Then someone blew one of those long, deep Tibetan horns, and my mind dissolved in bliss. I sat there for an indefinite period.

The monks were very kind when we got up from our meditations. Still in a somewhat altered state, I exited the temple onto the dusty road and walked around the simple town with Jack and a few Western friends. The smoke of cookfires in the late afternoon hit us, along with incense wafting out here and there from open temple doors, dust, and warm sunlight. People were milling everywhere. It was India.

We had heard that there was an old graveyard up the hill just behind the temples and thought we would do night meditation in the cemetery. We were drawn to this, as we had heard that it was a powerful tantric practice to meditate in graveyards at night and face your fears. At the time, this seemed like the perfect opportunity. I knew, however, that this would not be acceptable or even safe for a woman. So, before leaving, I dressed as a man wearing some of my husband's Indian clothing with a loose vest over it. I put my hair up, covered it with a turban, and went out with Jack and our friends to find this graveyard. It was late, almost midnight, when we quietly slipped out of the tent.

It was dark outside, with only a little moonlight, and the streets were mostly empty. People had settled in and were asleep for the night. We made our way through empty dirt roads to the side of the temples and up the hill until we came across what was clearly an ancient graveyard. It smelled dusty and dank, like old, rotting things. I began to worry if this was a place where thieves and cutthroats would hang out. In the moonlight, gravestones and broken things were lying about, with some old wagon to one side. I was uncomfortable, but we were there to meditate and face our fears, so I found a spot not too far from my husband and sat down to meditate.

There were sounds around. I couldn't tell if from people or animals. I worried about the cutthroats. It was hard to concentrate. I felt restless spirits in this old and unkept graveyard. It was scary, and my focus in meditation was not good, constantly shifting to sounds, smells, and noises. I wasn't doing a very good job of conquering my fears. It did not feel safe, and my antennas were up. After an interminable time trying to meditate, my friend began to whisper, "Let's get out of this place." The rest of us mumbled our assent and started to get up. By now, I was terrified and suspected my friends were too. It was a spooky, haunted graveyard. However, the good news was that we had not seen any cutthroats.

I looked around cautiously, as did others, and we began to exit, walking among the gravestones until we reached the dusty road and briskly walked back. I was incredibly relieved to be back in the shelter of the tent.

That was one adventure I did not want to repeat! I found the deep-red Oriental carpet I was sleeping on, pulled up my blankets, and fell sound asleep. After that, we stuck with meditating in temples and getting to know the wonderful Tibetan people camped all over Bodhgaya. A few days later, we headed back to the ashram.

The Primordial Guru

During the fall, while I was still in India, Anandamurti Baba gave some special teachings for daily life, and what I was told was an ancient sacred dance of Shiva called *Tandava*. He only gave formal talks, or darshan, once daily during this period. However, in the late evenings after dark, Baba would go to the central office and sit on the porch, teaching the monks the long-forgotten Tandava dance. He would watch and comment as they danced with torches and skulls in the dark of the night.

They were dark nights, with a blackout due to the Bangladesh war. It was very dark. No electric lights spoiled the night. The only light was from the torches held by the monks doing Tandava. On those special nights, my husband and I would come through a side opening to the porch and sit near Baba. There were not many people— only whoever happened to hear about Baba being there.

It was an ancient scene that felt timeless, as if it could have been enacted thousands of years earlier. There were the monks, their orange lungis tied up, legs bare, no shirts or shoes, arms outstretched, holding a skull in one hand and a torch in the other, dancing the dance of *Shiva*. Then there was the sound of ancient drums filling the night. Sitting quietly surveying the scene, golden skin glowing in the torchlight, making occasional comments, or giving instructions, Baba sat like Shiva, lord of the Universe. He seemed like a mountain before us. Enjoying himself teaching, laughing, and speaking with his sons, he was the iconic guru, lord Shiva manifest. Jack and I, Westerners sitting silently to his side in the dark, were perhaps the only aspect of the night that did not seem part of a far-distant past.

The Primordial Guru

An Important Teaching

It was late fall. We were back at the ashram, seeing Anandamurti Baba twice a day in darshan, when one day, a strong desire arose for me to give Baba a garland. I took a rickshaw to town and, after some effort, secured one. That night Baba gave darshan to a small group of us in the early evening outside the central office. I shyly brought my garland, wanting to be bold and give it to Baba myself to show my respect and love. There were only perhaps fifteen or so of us. We were standing in a semicircle around where Baba would sit. An orange-robed monk approached me and told me to give him the garland, and he would give it to Baba. I could not and would not give him the wreath. There was a strong feeling inside me that there could be no third party between me and Baba. It was not the nature of the bond between us. But this orange-robed monk refused to let me give this garland to Baba. Apparently, it was not proper for a woman to do.

I sat through darshan, garland in hand; my head bowed to hide the tears in my eyes. After Anandamurti Baba's talk, I returned to my room, garland still in hand, wounded in my heart. Baba was immediately there with me in subtle form, with kindness and compassion. I did *puja* and placed the garland around Baba's picture. In subtle form, my Baba graciously accepted my offering, given with all the love of my heart, now to Guru's inner form.

Yet to be turned aside from my physical guru, to feel he would not personally take a garland from me, hurt me bitterly. I had become desperately attached to the physical presence of Guru. I wanted to live my life in his magical, bliss-filled presence. My feelings were raw. I loved him and could not feel kindly towards anyone or anything that stood between us. I was hurt, and I was angry. He was my guru.

At the time, not having the advantage of the insight that comes with time and reflection, I saw it as the monk's fault. After all, it was a monk who would not let me give my garland. It was monks who tried to stop me from doing kirtan before Baba and from sitting in front of him. It was the monks who said I could not see Baba personally. Baba was always loving to me. To be in his presence was blissful. He showered me with his sweetness and never personally rejected me. So, my bitter feelings regarding my inability to be close to Anandamurti Baba got directed at the monks.

I could not see his guiding hand in their actions or understand why he did what he did. It has taken many years for me to see what happened with clarity and understanding. I knew it had symbolism but did not realize how significant it was until many years later, at Baba's death. When Baba would not take my garland as a physical guru, he left me with a choice of a secondhand relationship with him or to offer myself to his subtle form instead. He directed me away from his physical person. I realize, in retrospect, that he did this for my benefit and development.

Baba has his subtle ways of teaching. So, with one hand, he pushed me away; with the other, he caught me lovingly in his subtle form and set the course I was to follow. When I was forced to give my garland to my inner Baba, as a subtle guru, he sat before me and graciously accepted my offering. From that moment forward, this subtle guru would be the sole source of my spiritual guidance and the recipient of my love and service.

Something About Guru

Much of my personal experience has involved the subtle inner presence of the guru. I have also been blessed with seeing the guru manifest in physical form as Shrii Shrii Anandamurtijii, during this stay in India. Through these experiences of Baba, both as an inner guide and a physical guru, I have begun to understand the depth of the nature of guru.

In the classes at the Ashram, I learned that the term "guru" refers to a *mentor, guide, expert, or master* teacher. I was told that it translates to mean "one who brings light to the darkness." Traditionally, the first guru is often said to be the parents, then the child's schoolteacher, and finally a person's spiritual preceptor. It was commonly said by those around me in India that the ultimate guru is God or Brahma. Baba himself would say this in Darshan. A famous Yoga quote is, "Guru, God, and Self are One."

During this stay in India, I learned that "Baba" is often translated as Father and used in Sanskrit as an affectionate term to denote a holy man or spiritual leader. When my inner manifestation of guru first spoke to me, he said his name was "Baba." That is the name I have used ever since to refer to this inner spiritual manifestation of the Divine. I also call my physical guru, Shrii Shrii Anandamurti, Baba—so it is a bit confusing. My internal guru, my external guru, and many spiritual figures are all called Baba. Also, in its most esoteric definition, Baba denotes the divine Beloved.

Over time, I have come to see both my physical guru and my inner guru as manifestations of a larger aspect, as expressions of an archetypal divine Presence that is embodied in both forms. I have come to realize that whether the Divine comes to you as a man or a woman, a God or Goddess, an animal spirit, a tree, an inner guru or a burning bush, it is still the same God Self, the same Infinite Being dancing with you in the play of creation.

My Baba has often said to me that he is not a separate being but an aspect of the Cosmic mind, or *Mahat* in Sanskrit, manifesting through the *yoga maya*, or dance of creation of the cosmos. To me, he has been pure love, pure light, truth unbound, that which is beyond the mind— and then, again, my Baba, my guru, my mystic Beloved.

This time in India with, Shrii Shrii Anandamurti Baba, as a physical guru allowed the relationship I had forged with my inner guru, Baba, to continue and deepen. As I have said, this inner form of the guru, became the manifestation through which the love and teachings of truth would appear most deeply in my life. Yet, I had a passionate, undying love for Guru in his physical form.

Leaving

Sometime along the way, during my stay in India, my Baba began to promise me that he would see me in personal contact before my time with him as a physical guru was over. This helped me quite a bit. I was better able to tolerate the situation with this secret hope. I could enjoy the bliss of my time with Shrii Shrii Anandamurti in darshan. The subtle form of Guru was ever with me and ever loving.

Then one day before darshan, much to everyone's surprise, Baba called all of the women in the darshan hall into his personal contact room. There were ten or twelve of us. This was the first time he had had women with him in his private contact room. Many of the ladies, particularly the Indian women, were enraptured with looks of blessedness on their faces. But I was not in such a mood. I was upset. As a subtle guru, he had promised personal contact before he left. I knew this was it. I also knew he would be going and my time near him ending. Distressed by this knowledge and my desire to be near him, my upset with the inequities he posed between his treatment of men and women rushed to the surface.

I had never spoken to Anandamurti Baba during my time in India. Still, when he asked if anyone had any questions, I raised my hand, my brow furrowed with distress, and bluntly asked," Baba, why do you maintain sexist policies towards women?"

If he answered, it was evasive, and I no longer recall it. Something broke inside of me. All the pain I had been holding, feeling rejected because I was a woman, surfaced. I began wholeheartedly crying while insulting my guru. Then we were leaving, returning to the darshan room. I sat through darshan sobbing the whole time, a friend holding my hand. Deep inside, I knew it was the end. Knowing he would be leaving, I could only feel hurt, not reason. I was embarrassed that I had acted so badly.

I hoped that Baba was not angered or offended. He had not seemed angry, just evasive.

When I finally was alone, the subtle form of Baba came as always, assuring me that the physical guru, Anandamurti Baba, understood and held no anger towards me. I could not get over the pain. I was devastated, crying. I loved him, and I knew he would be leaving. My responses—awkward, foolish, and hurt—had arisen in the face of knowing deep inside that I was losing him.

Within a day or so, in the early morning before dawn, Baba was arrested and taken away from us. He was gone despite our hopes. I knew inside that it would be a long time before he came back. Early in the morning, when I found out he was gone, I went to my room, distressed. He was gone and had not said goodbye to me. After my outburst the other day, I felt things were unresolved. What we all dreaded had finally occurred. And so, I cried. I had lost my beloved guru without so much as a goodbye.

A friend came in to comfort me. When I told her of my wrenching distress, she laughed and said a man from Italy living at the ashram had had a dream that night about Baba and me. She encouraged me to talk to him. This grabbed my curiosity, so I got up and sought out this Italian devotee despite my inconsolable pain at losing Baba in form.

When I found him, I inquired about his dream. He smiled and told me in his strong Italian accent that he had indeed dreamed of me and Baba that very night. He said that in his dream, people were sitting around a dance floor when Baba approached me and took my hand to dance. In the dream, Baba drew me to him and, holding me close, began dancing. While dancing with me, Baba turned to this Italian man and said, "This is the dance of love."

I knew this was Baba's goodbye. I also knew it was real because it wasn't my dream but the dream of someone I barely knew. Baba knew me very well. He knew I was so skeptical about my own experiences; if the dream had been mine, I would have attributed it to subconscious desires or some such thing. But this Italian man had no motive to have such a dream. So, my skeptical mind could rest and conclude it was, in fact, Baba's loving goodbye and assurance of his forgiveness for my outburst, given with his typical subtlety.

Weeks went by after that, but Baba did not return. He was being kept near a remote village a few hours away. Eventually, Jack, I, and some other Western devotees went several times to try to see Baba in jail. We traveled by train and then by rickshaw to this remote village. It seemed the villagers had never seen Westerners before. By then, I was wearing a sari, a traditional Indian dress for women, but my long auburn hair still flowed free, and my fair skin and rosy cheeks were something new to these people, as was Jack's sandy hair.

Indian men swarmed our rickshaw chattering to us in the local language. It was all just noise to us. We could not understand them. One jumped on board the rickshaw, beaming a smile at us and waving his free hand around, yelling something we could not understand. Several others from the crowd joined him. I frowned and became worried they would overpower us. It got a bit dicey, but somehow, with our wild gesturing, they got the idea and backed off. To my relief, we got through the village—a collection of simple, earthy dwellings, with cookstoves, spicy Indian cooking smells, and lots of people.

We moved on to an abandoned temple by the side of the Ganges. We sat in that old, overgrown temple and we waited and waited, day after day. There was a mix of feelings on those long winter days while we were waiting. The temple, the monkeys, the vines that twisted around the old stone pillars, the smells of rainforest and dust, and the Ganges flowing wide below the hill were all part of something ageless, timeless. It amazed me and sent my mind and heart to some ancient, primordial place. The peace was enduring, the friendships sharing the experience, dear, but the pain of separation from Baba accompanied it. We could see the jail across the river, but they would not give us entrance.

Learning a Lesson

I had a friend in India who would joke that the only things lacking in the Indian diet were vitamins, minerals, and proteins. I also noticed that people around us didn't seem to have much of a concept of germs or how to avoid them. The chai shops, where you could catch a quick bite, would shoo the flies off the food before serving it to you on a plate rinsed in a five-gallon bucket of dirty water they had used all day to clean dishes. The truth was that in 1971, in the backwaters of India, any Westerner who stayed longer than six months tended to have health problems. People and cows defecated on the side of the roads daily, and the wells had walls about six inches high. When the rainy season would come, and the area would flood—well, you can imagine.

As I continued my stay in India, my health began to progressively deteriorate. I became thin and sickly, throwing up blood, and I grew weak. I was told I had amoebiasis, an amoebic dysentery that affects the liver. I took the medicines, but I kept losing weight and getting weaker.

I came to believe that my intense passion for spiritual states of consciousness and the deep blissful states I had been entering into in Baba's presence were more than my body could handle. My passion for liberation was great, but my body was not ready. I noticed that my health would improve when Baba went away for a week, as there was less Shakti. Due to my passion, the Shakti I was processing was too much for me.

Even the doctors finally concluded that it must somehow be related to my meditation. But I did not care. All I wanted was Baba. In my long hours of blissful meditation, my focus had become singular. I had lost interest in the material plane. I was spiritually focused. My passion was for the Divine, but my physical and mental bodies were wasting away in the process.

Finally, I became so ill that I needed to be hospitalized. They said I not only had amoebiasis but a serious kidney infection as well. The night I was taken to the hospital, I lay in bed wondering if I would die. In this state, I called to Baba in subtle form. There was no answer! He was not there for the first time since he had revealed himself to me. No matter how I pleaded, he would not respond to me.

There was only silence where his loving presence had been. Though I was seriously ill, my frail body as if lifeless, and pretty sure I was dying, he would not come to me the entire night. I figured out he was making a point—and making it strongly. I could not ignore it! I understood clearly that difficult night, languishing in an Indian hospital, that I had made a serious error. I was killing my body with my spiritual zealousness, and Baba did not approve.

My passion for the divine states of consciousness I was experiencing had become an all-consuming flame. But I learned from this experience, and from my inner Baba's rather sharp and unsympathetic lecture when he did come to me the next day, that I had to maintain my physical structure. I had lost all attachments to worldly life. I only wanted God, but with this lesson, I realized I had to develop worldly involvements.

I lived through that night and that lesson. I humbly submitted myself to my internal guru and vowed to turn myself around, to develop the physical and mental spheres. I vowed not to kill this body in spiritual passion, to maintain parallelism with the world around me.

From that point forward, I consciously set out to develop physical and mental attachments to hold my physi-

124

cal structure to this earth, as per my Baba's wishes. At the hospital, the doctors told me, "Go home to America, or you will die." I took this seriously. This was towards the end of my stay in India.

I likened my situation to a story Baba had told in darshan about a thief trying to catch the Buddha to pick his pocket. No matter how fast the thief ran, the Buddha was always one foot ahead. If the thief stopped, so did the Buddha. But if the thief then ran, the Buddha also ran, always the same distance away. If the thief ran faster to catch him, the Buddha would move faster. Nothing the thief did could change this. My longing for the Supreme was consuming, yet like the thief, I could not cross the distance between us by my own will, no matter what I did or how hard I threw myself into it.

I began to contemplate this along with the lesson about keeping my physical structure. I began to think that I needed to find a way to accept this worldly life and begin to see my Beloved within the changing patterns of creation. Perhaps, in that way, I could cross the gap. I began to think that rejection of being in the world was the fault preventing me from melting into his love. So, aligning with Baba's subtle instructions, I set my mind to grounding myself in the world and opening up to what this could teach me.

I would spend the next 18 years following the momentum this decision set in motion.

When I recovered a bit and came out of the hospital, back to the ashram, after some time, Jack and I began to have an intuitive feeling that we should leave. Baba was not coming out of jail, and the authorities would not let us see him. So, in March of 1972, we agreed it was finally time to go. We set out for Delhi, where we bought tickets for the U.S. Actually, we were supposed to have some sort of pass to leave the country, but we didn't know about it. Customs hassled us for a while at the airport because we did not have an "exit visa," but then allowed us to leave.

Jack and I did not find out until later, from friends still in Patna, that the authorities had a warrant for our arrest for questioning, as we were ashram managers, and the Indian government had recently banned Baba's community. It was a persecution of an entire spiritual community that the government later had to pay reparations for inflicting. Had we stayed longer or gone in for our "exit visas," we would have been arrested. We could not help but feel Baba's guiding hand in how we were taken out of danger, unaware it even existed.

Chapter VII
The Long Years Between

*A*s I flew back from India, the knowledge that I must form attachments in this world was foremost in my mind. I was being guided to do this, but my heart was with Baba and in mourning to be leaving him in his physical form. It was a heavy-hearted return, as if to an assignment I did not relish.

Landing in the United States in late March, I experienced more culture shock than I had felt when going to India. I was struck by all the neon lights, materialism, and lack of contact between people. The streets were empty—the people hidden in their isolated houses behind neatly mowed lawns. The States seemed far more foreign than India. As we were driven from New York to Philadelphia by some friends, looking out the window at the neighborhoods, barren of people, I truly once again felt like a stranger in a strange land.

We stayed with our Philadelphia friends for a few weeks, adjusting to being in the States, and then tried to make our way back to Chicago. After enduring a late blizzard, abandoning an immobilized car in the snow, and being stranded in a small Pennsylvania town, we finally got a ride from a man with a truck, followed by a long bus ride. We arrived in Chicago, cold and travel-worn, but we were back to a place we could live. I was delighted.

We soon rented an apartment on the Near North Side, a lovely brownstone flat on a quiet neighborhood street. We had the whole first floor. There were trees in front of our building, but the subway was only a half block away, and the sounds of the city were unavoidable. A few yogi types moved in; we called it an ashram and held public meditations. We also found jobs and began to support ourselves.

I was glad to have my own place again and for the luxury of lounging in a bed or on a couch. Though I was young, I was done with resting on a thin cotton sleeping bag and sitting on a cement floor with no backrest. I had taken the joys of Western comfort for granted until I didn't have them. Now they took on new meaning, and I appreciated this aspect of the West.

Yet in my meditations, my mind often wandered back to India, missing being in the presence of my guru, tears rising. Once again, as in my childhood, I felt alien in this big, metropolitan American city. My heart was still wounded by the loss of proximity to a divine Being in physical form, something I had longed for since childhood and had finally been fulfilled by Baba in India.

In subtle form, Baba remained with me, and I was making efforts to set my feet on the path my Baba had recommended, attempting to get involved and engaged with the world. By doing so, I hoped to keep my physical form healthy and alive and come to see the Divine in worldly life, something I had never experienced. It would take me a few years to form real attachments, and then the next 15 years to integrate them. At this time, living in Chicago, I was just going through the motions.

Then, within six months of settling in Chicago, friends from India invited us to come out to California to start a school for children. They offered us teaching positions. I was excited about this. I would be with the people I knew around Baba. This made me feel closer to Guru, and my inner Baba approved. So, we packed up, rented our place, and set out for California.

We stayed with my parents for a few days before leaving, and then when we said goodbye, my mom told me, "You may never see me again." I thought she was being overly dramatic and said, "Hey, Mom, don't worry, I'll come visit soon." She didn't say anything in return.

We set out on the adventure of driving once again in our old white Chevy, this time to Palo Alto, California, wherever that was. It was exciting. I had never been West. But when we arrived, I was told there was an urgent message. I needed to call home. When I called, I found out that my mother had died suddenly a few days after I had left. Getting off the phone, with my head in my hands and tears streaming, I just wanted to go home.

We flew back a few days later for the funeral, and my dad told me that my mother had had a dream the night before I left. In the dream, she was in our living room with my grandma and all the other family members who had passed on. She saw the legs of someone sitting in our recliner with her back turned. In the dream, Mom asked Grandma, "Who is that?" Grandma turned to her and said, "Don't ask." Then my mom knew that she was the one sitting in the chair, and the family was coming for her to take her with them. She had known when she said goodbye to me. She had known, and now I understood.

My stay in California started with this difficult loss, which, along with missing Baba in physical form, caused ongoing grief. We moved into an Oregon Street house with our friends when we returned to Palo Alto. A hippie, yoga community house rented by seven of us, it usually had at least twenty extra people staying there at any given time. It became so crowded that people would cover the living room floor at night and even sleep under the table.

But it was good *Sangha* (spiritual company), and we had a separate meditation room filled every morning with twenty or so people doing hours of meditation. That was really nice. There were several other houses like ours, making a great yoga and meditation community.

I enjoyed this community and was beginning to form attachments, but after a few months, mounting differences between Jack and me became so difficult that we decided to split up. Within a year, I lost my physical guru, my mother died, my husband left me, and I was still in poor health. Happiness slipped through my fingers like water. Emotional turmoil welled up and consumed me. Yet this time, it wasn't complete, as my inner guru was still with me, and I also got some unexpected help from another in the subtle realm.

One day as I went into overload and was falling apart with grief and loss, I tried to walk down the street but ended up sitting on a street corner, crying profusely. Suddenly, amid my tears, I felt the spiritual presence of Ramana Maharshi, a great Indian saint I had read much about but never met in person. He was there with me. His subtle body signature was distinct. It was not Baba. It was Ramana. Tears dried on my cheeks; I closed my eyes and felt the bliss of his appearance, uplifting my mind out of sorrow into the love of this beautiful healing presence. I thanked him with all my heart and walked home in a spiritual state, feeling his being around me. I have felt deeply connected to him since. He has come again at other times over the years.

Besides Baba, he and Anandamayi Ma, a well-known Indian Master, said to fall into divine states for days at a time, have come to me the most often. I've also never met Anandamayi Ma in physical form, but her subtle form has come to me many times during kirtans and chants. I could feel her love and holy presence wash over me as I meditated, leaving a trail of bliss.

Back at Oregon Street, I tried to practice what I thought was the solution to my spiritual difficulty, to develop my physical and mental spheres. I found my personality an unworkable medium. I would feel one thing, but another would come out when I went to speak or act. I did not know how to maneuver the world, but I thought learning how was what Guru wanted. It was a hard road that first year after India.

Yet my Baba stayed with me, still the love of my life. When I was ill, Baba would sit next to me on the bed in a subtle form. He would care for me and speak words of comfort. When I was in fear or emotional pain, he often had words of wisdom or solace. He would advise me on my psychological problems. One time when I was in the middle of a scary nightmare, he entered my mind and said, "Wake yourself up. You are dreaming." Such was his care, to even pull me out of a bad dream. My mind would stray to him, here and there during the day, and I would fall into moods of bliss.

Family and Attachments

I was still living at the Oregon Street house—Jack had moved out, and we were getting divorced—when the man who would become my husband for the rest of my life and father to my children moved in. Dressed in yogi whites, with sandy-colored hair and a big beard, he came in, and everyone immediately asked him to sing some devotional songs. Apparently, he already had a reputation as a musician. His name was Liam, and when he sang, his voice was like heaven. His music put everyone in a spiritual mood, and I fell in love.

We soon lived together and, by 1977, were married. I was in a graduate program getting my Ph.D. in Transpersonal Psychology and working part-time when, in 1979, we had our first child. By then, I was indeed attached, grounded, and fully living in the world. I had done as my guru had asked. I had formed attachments. Now I was so attached that I had difficulty finding time for my meditation. I had gone from meditating most of the day to barely being able to catch a half hour here or there. Our hippie days were gone. We owned a house with a half-acre of beautiful gardens, had a family, a second child, and a very busy life.

My Liam   Our Beautiful Sons

Yet spiritual life did continue during these busy family years. My inner Baba stayed with me—guiding, consoling, and teaching me. Then when my father's time came to leave this world, Baba did something pretty amazing.

Passing Over

Liam and I were living in downtown Palo Alto on Channing Street when my dad became ill. We went back to Illinois for a few weeks to be with him. He was in a care facility at the time. I could not do much to assist, and we soon had to return to our lives in California. Saying goodbye was difficult; I knew I would never see him again.

I had read a book about Milarepa, a great Tibetan yogi, that described Milarepa helping his mother transition at the time of her death. So, knowing I couldn't do much for my dad but wanting to help, I got the idea to ask my inner guru, Baba, if he would please help my father when he passed. Baba kindly agreed and said he would assist when the time came.

I had been back home from my visit to my dad for a month or so when my brother called to say my father was dying. I immediately went to meditate, sending my mind to Chicago, to my dad's room. I began to visualize or "see" the room, but I could not feel my father there. He didn't seem to be there. Then in my inner vision, I saw Baba enter the room I was sitting in; he appeared to my right, and my father was standing next to him.

Baba was dressed in his usual Indian whites, and my dad was wearing a plaid work shirt, his wavy black hair streaked with grey, as it had been when I last saw him. There was a feeling about Baba, that he had come to show me he was keeping his word and for me to say a quick goodbye to my dad, but that he could not stay for long. In my father, I saw confusion. He had been an atheist, and this was all out of his reality, but he was going along without fighting it, in a resigned state of mind. I said goodbye to him, and Baba left, my father in tow.

Going back to Chicago for the funeral and talking to family, they told me that Dad had gone through a change the last few days before he died. He had stopped fighting and become resigned and passive, just as I had seen when Baba brought him to me.

I never felt my father's presence after that. His spirit was gone. Whatever Baba had done, my dad seemed to cross over cleanly and swiftly. I will ever be grateful for Baba's kindness to my father.

Spiritual life

As the years passed, Liam and I raised our children and worked to support our family. We also stayed active in our spiritual community, attending retreats and weekly meditations. However, my all-consuming passion for my divine Beloved slowly cooled a bit. I had formed the attachments he had guided me to, but now those dominated my mind, and my heart was being pulled away from Baba. He still was with me and my love with him, but our connection gently cooled as the years went on and a long stretch unfolded of grounding in the world.

I had some prophetic dreams, we continued our meditation, Baba stayed with me in subtle form, and Liam and I made a habit of seeing any spiritual masters who came to our area. Without Anandamurti Baba physically present, we felt guided to one and then another guru. Liam and I found solace and spiritual inspiration from the various spiritual masters. Yet Baba continued to be our *Ista Deva*, our heartfelt guru. We felt he allowed us to meet various saints and sages to guide us in the long years of his physical absence and deepen our meditation.

Not long after settling into our home in Palo Alto, we heard through the grapevine that a guru named *Swami* Muktananda had recently started giving darshans at someone's house in the Berkeley Hills. So, we got directions and set off to check him out.

We came to this rather lovely house in Berkeley and were ushered into a relatively large room where we sat on the floor with many other people. Soon Swami Muktananda arrived and sat in a big chair in a corner up front. He looked like a bit of a character with his casual orange robes and gingerly walk, carrying a peacock feather. It turned out he would use this peacock feather to touch people's heads and give them *Shaktipat*, his spiritual blessings. He had a powerful spiritual presence. So, we listened to his talk, and as he went around the room, swatting people with his peacock feather, we received our blessings as well. It was quite beautiful. After he touched me with his peacock feather, a wave of ecstatic bliss flowed from my head through my body. I felt he had indeed given me his blessings.

We continued to see Swami Muktananda over the years as he settled into his ashram in Oakland. We even went to one of his retreats. He got to know us and helped us in Anandamurti Baba's absence. One time in one of his large darshans, Liam stood up, raised his hand, and asked about Baba being in jail. Muktananda said, "He's not in jail; you are. He is *Taraka Brahma* (the point between the manifest and unmanifest universe). He is always free."

Another time, several of us invited him to visit Anandamurti Baba's ashram in Los Altos Hills, and he said yes! We were delighted. He came to our place, sat down in a big chair we provided, and said, "Your Baba is very fortunate to have such devotees as you. You do him honor." After that, he gave a small talk and blessed us with his peacock feather.

Mt. Shasta Mystics

From the beginning of my stay in Palo Alto, California, I kept hearing of Mt. Shasta and how the White Brotherhood of Ascended Masters met inside the mountain. Friends were all about it and kept telling me I had to go. They said there was this lady there named Pearl that I had to see. She channeled the ascended masters. Also, Godfrey Ray King, who wrote of Saint Germain and the Ascended Masters, was connected to Mt. Shasta and had a center there.

So, off Liam and I went to Mt. Shasta with friends in what must have been the early '70s. When we got there, we camped at Wagon Camp, a hard-to-reach area, wild and untouched, on a stream halfway up the mountain. We stayed for weeks just living on the mountain, hearing the stories about the flying saucers landing, sightings of the little people on the mountain, and the Lemurians, a tall race of fair-haired people from an ancient lost continent. They said Mt. Shasta was once a part of Lemuria. Then the stories about the ascended masters and their meetings topped it off. It was magical! The sunlight, fresh mountain air, crystal-clear water in the stream, and the profound white peaks before us—the air shimmered with high energy! Meditation was powerful on the mountain. For me, it was Shiva's mountain, our Himalayas of the West. And Baba—Baba was there.

Periodically during this stay, we all gathered together and made our way off the mountain, a challenging task, to go to town and see Pearl. We gathered in her humble living room, a bunch of spiritual mountain hippies sitting on her rug as she sat in a chair and called in the various Ascended Masters. "It is El Morya. He has entered the room and has a message for you...." "Now Saint Germain has come...." Like this, master after master would visit us as we sat on the floor of her living room. I would feel each presence, each one slightly different from the other, but there was such high energy from the mountain and meditation that everything felt magical. We met each moment with wonder and awe.

To clarify, we were all yogis and vegetarians and did not do any kind of drug or alcohol. We followed a strict yogic lifestyle. The high and the awe were just natural, a result of the amazing energy on Mt. Shasta and our long hours of meditation, not to mention a few Ascended Masters. Needless to say, we made many trips over the years with friends to the mountain, sometimes for a weekend and others to stay and live on the mountain for weeks. We often listened to Pearl bring in the masters and had our own mystical experiences on the mountain. Though things have changed, and the mountain has been discovered, to this day it is my shelter on the planet, my sacred place.

One of my favorite places to stay was at Panther Meadow. At close to 9,000 feet, it is only usable for a few months of the year. So, during the hot months, we would go up to the upper meadow and camp. Back in the early years, there would be few other people there.

On one trip, Liam and I went alone to camp in the upper meadow, making our beds in a rock shelter just above the tree line and the sacred spring that gushes out of the rocks near the top of the clearing. We stayed for a few weeks, entirely alone up there. No one else was in the meadow. I dressed in an Indian lungi, a kind of wrap-around cloth, carried a tall staff, and meditated most of the day. We slept in the open under the stars. At night the stars were magnificent, brilliant as can only be seen at such altitudes. They took our breath away.

Yet this one night, it was a bit cloudy when we went to sleep. Then sometime during the night, we awoke to thunder, lightning, and rain pelting us. Liam and I got up quickly and looked around. The bright lightning flashes hitting the ground around us illumined everything, but the problem was that we were above the tree line and, therefore, the tallest objects around. Like lightning rods, we stood out in the night. No one else was around, and we were too far from our car to make it there, so we ran down to where some stunted trees grew and cowered down next to them, trying to be small and not a pair of lightning rods.

After we spent twenty minutes or so getting drenched and feeling terrified, the storm finally moved on. Everything was soaked, especially us, but we dried off as best we could, found some almost dry ground, and went back to sleep. Arising the next morning to clear mountain air shimmering with energy, the magical spring overflowing, and the crystal-clear stream running through the meadow of wildflowers, we felt gratitude to the mountain and to the divine forces at work protecting us and guiding us.

Guru Bawa

A few years after we first met Muktananda, we heard of another master who had come to town. His name was Guru Bawa. He was a frail, fragile-framed *Sufi* guru with the snow-white hair of an aged man but a face as clear and young as one 29 or 30 years old. As the story goes, one day, he had just walked out from behind a boulder in front of a group of people on a pilgrimage. He was an old, old man with no past, from nowhere anyone knew of, speaking an unknown language. The people taught him their language, but when they would ask him where he was from, every time, he would talk about the origins of the universe. There seemed to be no separate self to have a history. He was a mystery.

The first time we saw him, we were struck by his purity and simplicity. Ageless, with his young face, snow-white hair, and fragile body, dressed in white, he seemed otherworldly. It was as if a being of pure light had just appeared before us; folding his arms across his heart in a gesture of pure love, he captivated us. My heart beamed in his presence. He was so beautiful, just made of love and light, literally, with the innocence of a small child.

His darshans were small, maybe 30 or 40 people, and afterward, he would come up to each person and hug them. He was light-embodied, barely human. I loved this simple and holy man. The bliss that poured from him was unbelievable. To be in the presence of such a being was a great boon to my meditation. He came now and then to our area for some years, and we continued to see him each time he came.

Guru Bawa

Swami Muktananda

Sister Palmo

Tharthang Tulku
Rinpoche

The Tibetans

At some point in the early 1980's, we also met Tarthang *Tulku*, head of the *Nyingma* lineage in Tibetan Buddhism, and Sister Palmo, a long-time student of the *Karmapa* and renowned Tibetan teacher, credited with being the first Western woman to take full ordination in Tibetan Buddhism.

Tarthang Tulku had a center in Berkeley, just across the Bay, so when we heard about him, Liam and I decided to visit. We had studied Tibetan Buddhism a bit and resonated with it as a tantric path. It seemed similar to Baba's path, classic North Indian tantra, so we thought it would be good to see him and check it out. When we went, we liked him and started going to his programs for some months. We got to know Tarthang Tulku a bit from this, and while we were talking with him one day, it came out that Liam and I were artists. He liked this and asked us to illustrate some children's books for him, which we did.

Then one day, as we were meeting about the books, we casually asked about Shrii Shrii Anandamurti Baba, our guru, and all the political trouble in India we did not like or understand. He simply cautioned, "Don't throw out the baby with the bathwater." Over the years, I have come to realize the power of this simple but compelling advice. We highly respected the Tulku and took his advice to heart, realizing we should keep holding on to Baba and his teachings while forgetting about the organization and the politics of India. We appreciated his guidance.

Meditation was good at the Tulku's programs, and we respected him greatly as a lineage holder.

Then we happened upon Sister Palmo. She was a British elder who had been a Tibetan nun for many years. Sister Palmo was a robust woman who dressed in burgundy robes and spoke with a bit of a British accent. She taught Tibetan Buddhism to students in a nearby South Bay town. Hearing about her, we began to attend her talks on a regular basis.

Liam and I had been attending her talks and studying with her for some months when, one day after a meeting, she took us aside and asked if we wanted to receive a transmission and become students of Tibetan Buddhism. She noted we would then be part of the Sangha and not just visitors. The idea of being a part of a community appealed to both of us, yet we declined, despite the temptation. For both Liam and me, Baba was, first and foremost, our only guru, even if we could not be around him physically.

Though we sat with many masters and participated in many communities, we were always outsiders, which was difficult. We wanted to belong. I wanted to belong, but I also knew that despite the spiritual blessings and bliss I felt around various masters, Baba was the love of my life, my Kula Guru, my home, even if I was without Sangha.

Visitation by an Ascended Master

It was shortly after our time with the Tibetan masters that I had a profound and very significant dream, if, indeed, it can be called a dream.

A friend is selling tickets at a theater house. She is smiling, as if she knows something I am about to find out. I go to the window, buy a ticket, and walk inside. Next thing I know, I am in my actual dining room where I live on Channing Street, with the built-in wooden cabinets and antique table. I am sitting on a dining room chair.

Standing before me is a tall, thin man dressed in something akin to Middle Eastern clothing. He is wearing a robe of sorts covered by a vest. He appears to be European in skin tone and features, with sandy hair and no beard. He begins speaking and proceeds to tell me he is from the White Brotherhood, a group of mystical ascended masters.

He then says to me, "We will be testing you." I am wondering what this means. He continues by saying something about "... to be accepted by us." When I think, "How will I know if I pass your test?" I get back an energetic response equivalent to, "Don't call us; we'll get in touch if we choose to."

Then he tells me he will show me something about myself. It seems as if this is being done to prove to me that this experience is real—or perhaps to give me some information—or both. Regardless, this ascended master then touches me on the forehead, and somehow the knowledge arises in my awareness that I have intentionally taken on all of the emotional pain and suffering I have endured. This understanding arises for the first time. With it, awareness dawns that I have taken this on to gain more understanding and compassion for the emotional suffering of others. A profound feeling comes, though I do not know what to think of this. The moment passes. I look up. He is gone.

For the first time in my life, I sit straight up in bed after a dream. Instantly wide awake, sitting in my bed, I wonder, "Did I just have a dream or a visitation?"

To this day, I have never had a follow-up visitation by an ascended master to let me know if I passed their test. Yet this dream, in its own way, was a foretelling of the work I would be guided to do as my destiny unfolded in the far future from this prophetic dream. I have often wondered, if I had not passed their test, would I have been later called to the work? I do not know.

More Gurus

As those long years between one spiritual opening and another passed, and I learned to live in the world, there were many gurus we went to meet. Fortunately, in those days, there was quite an array of Indian masters moving through the San Francisco Bay Area.

In addition to the gurus already mentioned, we spent time with Shri Chinmoy, who walked out of a darshan we attended with hundreds of people. Apparently, he got offended by the audience. Then there was Chinmayananda Saraswati, a very learned Sanskrit scholar whom Liam and I enjoyed seeing. We went to see him each time he came to the Bay Area and got to know him personally over time.

Kirpal Singh, a Sikh master, was another figure we enjoyed seeing whenever he visited the Bay Area. He always wore a white turban and shirt with a dark-colored suit jacket over it and had a long, saintly white beard. He spoke in a low, hypnotic voice, giving words of spiritual wisdom. As with most of the Masters, we felt a deep spiritual vibration around him that put us in bliss-filled states of mind.

One darshan stands out because, while he was speaking to an audience of hundreds of people, I felt he was looking at me for a long time. I couldn't figure out why. I even looked behind me, thinking there must be someone else he was looking at, but it seemed he was looking at me for some reason.

Then a year or so later, I was sitting in a doctor's waiting room when I suddenly felt his presence come into the room. It was intense and lasted for some time. I didn't understand it. I am not his devotee. However, a few days later, I found out he had passed away on the very afternoon I had sensed his presence, perhaps in his leaving. I wondered why I had these experiences with him. Maybe there was some connection I didn't know about, or somehow, we just met on the spiritual level. I never found out.

Sometime later, Liam and I went to see the Karmapa doing the Black Crown Ceremony. A powerful being, something about him reminded me of Baba. Then we went to a lecture by Chögyam Trungpa Rinpoche, who showed up an hour late and drank sake during his talk, getting tipsier as the night went on.

One of our favorite people to visit was Swami Satchidananda. He was a saintly, orange-robed swami we would go to see in the attic of his San Francisco ashram in the early 1970s. We would climb this narrow, seemingly rickety staircase and find a place on the attic floor. There would be some kirtan chanting, and then this lovely swami would come in, slightly bent over, as the attic was not quite tall enough to walk through. I felt bliss around him.

Baba Hari Dass, at Mount Madonna in Watsonville (near Monterey), became a part of our lives for many years. He was a silent yogi we'd known and loved from when he first came in the seventies until his passing in 2018. We first saw him at a private house, Ma's house, long before the Mount Madonna retreat center existed. He never talked but wrote on a chalkboard to give wisdom and answer questions. Highly knowledgeable about Yogic philosophy and teachings, he had a beautiful, deep vibration. He started the Mount Madonna Community, which remains a spiritual haven and center for wisdom teachings to this day. He was a shelter in the storm for Liam and me when, for some years, we were Baba's devotees but without spiritual community.

We went on a retreat in Mt. Shasta with Kennett Roshi, a British Zen master, which was informative and unique for us. She was an excellent teacher, but the tradition was foreign to us. Interestingly, years later, when I was attending the Institute of Transpersonal Psychology, she gave a week-long intensive as part of my graduate program. A buxom woman in black Zen Master robes, she taught us the tea ceremony and the basics of Zen.

Then a bit later, there was Mother Meera in her silent darshans and "Amma," Mātā Amritānandamayī Devi, the hugging saint from whom we have received many hugs and much loving guidance over the years. In her darshans and retreats, I have felt spiritual energy and states of bliss in her presence. In Baba's physical absence, she has gifted me with spiritual waves, profound states of consciousness, and some practical advice.

All these masters have helped us along our spiritual paths in one way or another and boosted our meditations. Some emanated such bliss-filled light that it uplifted us into divine states in their presence. The grace of exposure to such energies has been a great boon.

Anandamayi Ma

Hari Das Baba

Ramana Maharshi

Swami Satchidananda

Kirpal Singh

Amma - Mata Amritanandamayi

Another Dream

Years before the destiny I had mused about as a child unfolded, I had another powerful dream that stood out to me. Calling me with a feeling that was profound and expansive, it was one of those special dreams emerging from a deeper place within.

It begins. I am running with wild horses. I am running next to one horse that is white and spotted like an Appaloosa. As we run together, I feel the freedom and wildness of the experience, the wind blowing in my face, the horse's mane, and my hair flying in the wind. It is unbelievable freedom and pure joy.

The scene shifts, and I am standing in front of a wide turbulent river I know I must cross. The sky is dark with clouds as restless as the river. There is a small boat in front of me that I need to take to cross the deep waters. I get into the boat and begin to row. The waters are dark and dangerous. In the dream, I am now a man dressed in robes. I row with all my strength, knowing I must cross these deep and dangerous waters. I must get to the other side. Heart in my throat, I look down into the dark, swirling water. It is better not to. I keep rowing.

Finally, after hours of struggle, with a sigh of relief, I reach the other side and get out of the boat. I have crossed the deep waters and I am on the farther shore. Now, still a man, I am a shepherd dressed in shepherd's robes with a shepherd's staff. I see a flock of sheep before me. I move amongst them, and they surround me. I feel I am where I need to be. I am their shepherd. I walk amidst them, with robes and staff, knowing I have reached the other side—and that I am where I am supposed to be.

At the time, I did not understand this dream. Still, I felt the high spiritual energy that accompanied it, and as with the ascended master encounter, I somehow knew inside it was telling me something important.

Transitions

As the years passed, these dreams came from time to time. Liam and I continued to seek the company of Masters, I did what meditation I could with my busy family life and professional career, and I kept learning from and being comforted by Baba's inner presence. Baba was not only a source of comfort and advice, but also taught me the ancient teachings of yoga through spiritual states, realizing truths, and long hours explaining teachings. Many yogic teachings I learned from him and only later read in books. Much of my knowledge has come to me firsthand from Baba's subtle form.

Yet as time went on, spiritual states became less frequent than in the early days of meditation. During this time, the intense and painful longing for closeness to the Divine became an underground stream that never entirely vanished but receded to protect me from the intensity of my feelings, which I did not know how to resolve. My mind was immersed in the world. I still wondered about my sense of destiny as a child. Yet I had decided to go ahead and get married and have kids. I couldn't figure out how that sense of destiny related to my life, except in these rare dreams.

Baba was still with me, but I was distracted by my daily life. He had guided me to hold on to this world and learn to be happy in it. Now I didn't know how to detach. All the scriptures talk about the detachment that is needed for spiritual life. I wondered why Guru had guided me to become so immersed in the world. It was not until many years later that I fully understood this life lesson: that nothing needs to be rejected. It is all one and the same, inseparable, immortal, eternal being, in the play of form and formless, in the world and in Guru.

Quickening of Sadhana

It was, perhaps, in the winter of 1988 that Baba came to me and began saying, "You are like a person betwixt and between two worlds. You have one foot in the world and one with the Divine." He told me that this is a painful position, as I cannot be happy in the world, knowing too much of the Sublime and yet unable to fulfill my longing. He said, "I will help you."

After that, many things started shifting. My meditation began to improve. Blissful states began to come again more frequently. I began to experience seeing God in all creation. This started when I saw the movie, *"The Last Temptation of Christ."* I don't know exactly what it was about the film that stirred me so profoundly; perhaps Christ's feeling when hearing God speak to him, not knowing if he was crazy, drove my mind deep.

When in the film, Jesus said that he pitied—meaning loved—all creatures, my mind went out in love with all those in the theater. When the movie ended, I was in a deep state of love, barely able to get up and walk, unable to talk. All was the form of God. All woven together in love. I was in all creation, and all was God. This state lasted for two or three weeks after the film. Every molecule, every atom, every object was the absolute perfect form of God, of Baba—and it was also me. I was indivisible from him in his manifest form, this manifest Universe. This state caused me some pain, even though it was beautiful. I wanted to give it to others, to give others a direct experience. It needed to be shared. But I did not know how to share it.

With this experience, I began to feel a tremendous desire to complete the process of my sadhana. Like the Buddha, I wanted to sit down somewhere, draw my circle, and not get up until I either died or became fully enlightened. But I also felt the draw of my duty to family and worldly job to help support my family. So, with great pain, I put aside my spiritual longing and kept my duties, knowing I could not continue to make that choice. Slowly, after some weeks, this experience of all-being Divine form faded.

This state was reawakened when I began attending *Dharmachakras*, or community meditations. Through several people whose children were friends with mine, I was drawn to go back to these weekly meditations at the local ashram. One day, while attending meditation, I looked at Baba's picture, and his energy was so strong I was overpowered. I just sat there in front of his picture in a blissful state.

Soon, I began to have deep experiences of Baba's presence at every collective meditation I attended. Many times, I knew that even if he were physically present, he could be no closer. I felt him in my own body, in the cells of my body. I felt that he was there with me at that moment—not in India. All things, all manifestations, would become his form.

When I would rise from meditation, I would not come out of this state. I would drive home in an intoxicated state with bliss pouring through me, the perception of all manifestations as his form firmly established without effort. The veil was lifted from my perception. This state would last for two or three days, slowly dissipating as I externalized my mind in my work and family. I wanted to hold to it, but I knew it could not be clutched at. I knew I had to do my worldly duties and that it would come again. Every Sunday during this period, when I would go to Dharmachakra and look at Baba's picture, this would occur.

Each week there would be a slightly different emphasis in this exquisite state, which would last after meditation and into the week. Baba continued his sweet dialogue with me. The association of these states with going to Dharma Chakra lasted for about six months. By then I was, of course, completely enthused about attending collective meditations.

I was aware during this phase that I was experiencing the blessedness of his bliss and his form but that the deeper samadhi—the formless samadhi, or absorption—was evading me. During one Dharma Chakra, after sadhana, I got up in a very deep and blessed mood and went to Baba's picture. His energies poured forth from the picture as they were wont to do.

I looked into him, my beloved guru, the depths of his being opening before me. Looking into a well of exquisite and sincere love, everything in me wanted to move into the depths of that well. He was open and willing to accept me. But as much as I would match his love, I could not go very far before I hit a brittleness in my own mind, an inability to give, to surrender in the deep love he was revealing to me.

This was difficult for me. Everything in me wanted to move with him into the well of his being. I wanted to go so deep into this honesty that, like the salt doll dropped into the sea, I could dissolve my being into the vast ocean that is Guru and lose myself in his depths. But I could not go very far before I had to say to my Beloved, "My Lord, I would follow you into the depths of love, but I am prevented against my desire by the poverty of my mind. I am so sorry." He, in his kind way, had only comfort for me, only sweet and soothing words.

This experience became a sadhana for me and made a deep impression in my mind. It created a vision of his love's sincerity and purity, which I kept recalling. It began to move me the way a pole star would. I began to understand that the process is not to follow the light inward in sadhana but to follow that authentic and human quality of love inward to the depths. I began to discover that it requires a willingness for a very real, personal, and total self-disclosure. There can be no walls to hide behind, no holding back.

Finishing a Cycle

In February of 1990, I received my license as a clinical psychologist. When I finally finished this last, arduous test and completed all my professional requirements, I discovered I had absolutely no professional desires. Everyone said, "You must be so happy!" but I was just happy not to have to jump through any more hoops.

I felt an eighteen-year cycle of my life coming to an end. I had chosen to study transpersonal psychology because I wanted to do psycho-spiritual work. I tried to find a way to express my relationship and love for Baba and the realizations I had in my work. But now I felt the pressure of my spiritual life, which I had been holding at bay to devote myself to the academic rigors of completing my Ph.D. and licensing exam. Now I only wanted to be lost in the depths of love with my beloved Baba.

Chapter VIII

Sacred Passages

With the quickening of sadhana that began in 1988, my life changed. I was a mom with two young boys and had a part-time job working as a psychologist at a state hospital. Needless to say, I was busy. But I was also being drawn into my sadhana, spending every moment I was not required to do something in meditation.

My physical guru, Shrii Shrii Anandamurti Baba, left his body in October 1990, the same year I received my license. Before and during the time between these events, I began to experience a profound spiritual opening.

Light in My Palms & Feet

During this period, a change began to occur in my inner communion with Baba, the dance of his expression shifting, weaving in my mind and heart the sweet flow of the Beloved. He began to open my heart to a depth of love previously unknown to me. The brittleness I had encountered in myself in my earlier experience began to soften. My inhibitions began to dissolve, my resistance to dissipate. In a bond of love so deep I cannot put it into words, the awakened Shakti energies moved upward into my heart.

Then one day, while I was lost in meditation, a pure white lotus began to form and bloom in my heart, filling me with a nectarean, sacred love. I saw light flowing from the magnificent heart lotus through subtle channels of my body, opening chakras in the palms of my hands and the soles of my feet. My palms and soles began to glow with pure white radiance. I could feel the open chakras. The radiance felt holy, sacred. It was as if a wave of grace was moving from the lotus blooming in my heart, through my body, into my hands and feet, and then out into the world. I felt as if, should I touch someone, this great blessing would touch them as well.

The experience of this sacred white radiance in my heart, and in my palms and the soles of my feet, became constant for almost a year. Often in meditation, I saw golden channels stemming from the central column in my spine, flowing to my arms, legs, and other parts of my body. Beautiful lotus flowers bloomed within each chakra, and a Sanskrit letter would appear on each petal.

When all this began, doubt and uncertainty about following internal teachings tugged at me. With gentle compassion, Baba would carefully untie the knots in my mind, his words and explanations coming with their usual loving kindness and logic until I understood and could accept what he was showing me.

I began to feel that every particle of the Universe is only the form of my Beloved and is my own form. I began to experience this body and mind as no longer mine, belonging instead to the Beloved of my heart, to the one eternal essence of being, dancing with me in the play of creation as my Baba.

I lie upon the couch.
My head resting in Your lap.
Immersed in the feel of you.
Rain softly falls outside my window.

My heart is a radiant white light.
I feel my palms and feet.
Aglow and alive with shimmering light
The force of this energy moves my hands.
For its expression

Ecstatic flows move up and down my spine.
Sensual sensations in rivers of light

Dreamily I enjoy Your companionship.

Sacred Marriage

As the summer progressed, the focus of my meditation experience drew more to the depths. The allegory of the sacred marriage to the Divine began to find full enactment in my sadhana. In deep and extended meditations, as the play of divine consciousness unfolded, my inner guide began to manifest as the divine Beloved.

Then one day, in a mystic ceremony in the depths of meditation, he united us in a sacred marriage of the small self to the Beloved.

I am sitting quietly alone in my meditation room. The house is empty. I am already in a blissful mood. Baba is there in a subtle form. Pure love emanates from him, a glow that has already unstrung my heart.

I sit before him in the depths of my inner vision. I am lost in love and grace. He draws upon my forehead a mark extending from Ajna Chakra to Sahasrara, the third eye to the top of my head. As he does this, an overpowering white radiance and a blessedness fill my mind. My heart melts. He tells me this is the marriage of my small self to the Infinite One and that I will never be the same. That this is forever.

On the soles of my feet, symbols appear, drawn in red, of mystic eyes. I melt into the pure white light that stuns the mind with intolerable love and am lost in union with the Beloved of my heart.

Melded with him, I feel every particle of my being is infused with my Beloved. The atoms and cells of my body, my mind, and the world around me become the form of my Baba, of my divine Beloved. There is nothing outside of this ecstatic love. I see the Beloved of my heart manifest in every particle of existence. Inner and outer lose distinction as I become lost in Cosmic love.

In this sacred dance, my Baba showered unreserved and profound love upon me, showing this small one the nature of real love, of which human love is only a reflection. I was touched beyond words, feeling deeply connected to my mystic Beloved and the dance that unfolded.

You stand before me.
Husband of my heart
The light of your essence
Softly dissolving the
Boundaries between us

Thou art within and without
Formed and Formless
Lover, love, and Beloved
Thou art personal and tender
Yet vast as an endless ocean

Your touch caresses me,
Leaving me intoxicated with Your presence.
Immersed in Your sweet radiance,
I am fulfilled.

Thus, my experience unfolded, but it was not until years later in my readings that I came to understand that the mystical marriage has been a part of the experiences of those who love the Divine in spiritual traditions of various religions throughout history. The mystical marriage to the Goddess is part of Judaism. As part of esoteric Christianity, nuns and often mystics become the brides of Christ. In Hinduism, *Radha* and *Krishna*, *Shiva* and *Parvati*, *Rama* and *Sita* enact the soul's journey to unity with the Divine. In all traditions, the mystic marriage denotes the state of a human soul living intimately united to God through grace and love.

Of course, I did not know of this at the time. I don't know if my experiences were as profound as those described in the writings I have read, but the writings of saints, poets, and sages have helped me to understand that other people, deeply in love with the Divine, have also had this experience. I do know that this sacred union never comes from human striving but through giving of oneself to the Beloved and the shower of grace of that Divine One.

Saint Teresa of Ávila (1515–1582) expresses her experience beautifully in her writings in the *Interior Castle*:

"The big and hidden secret is this: an infinite God seeks and desires intimacy with the human soul. Once we experience such intimacy, only the intimate language of lovers describes the experience for us: mystery, tenderness, singularity, specialness, changing the rules "for me," nakedness, risk, ecstasy, incessant longing, and of course also, necessary suffering."

Many explain this love in poetry, as it is so hard to put into words the love of the heart. St. John of the Cross writes in *The Spiritual Canticles*:

I lost myself. Forgot myself.
I lay my face against the Beloved's face.
Everything fell away, and I left myself behind,
Abandoning my cares among the lilies, forgotten.

Kabir also tells of this love in the *One Hundred Poems of Kabir*, translated by Rabindranath Tagore.

A sore pain troubles me day and night, and I cannot sleep.
I long for the meeting with my Beloved,
And my father's house gives me pleasure no more.
The gates of the sky are opened, the temple is revealed:
I meet my husband and leave at His feet the offering of my body
and my mind.

After this profound experience, I was curious to know what the symbols that I saw on my feet meant, so a few months later, I asked Baba Hari Dass, whom I knew to be very scholarly. I showed him a drawing of the mystic eyes, and he told me, like *Om*, it is the symbol of *Shabda Brahman*, the Brahma of sound. I later read in Yogapedia that Shabda Brahman is transcendental sound, as outlined in the *Vedic* scriptures. In Sanskrit, Shabda means "sound" or "word," and Brahman is "Supreme Self" or "Absolute of the Universe." Ancient scriptures centering on yogic philosophies state that sound and God are the same and that "Every substance is made up of vibrations (subtle sound)."

This explanation of the mystic eyes as symbols of Shabda Brahman made sense to me, as my Baba manifests through inner sound. His love emanates through the inner voice. Even his outer voice, when I am giving his talks or "Baba talks," carries his vibrational presence in the sound of the words. So, with this explanation, I felt complete. It deepened my understanding of my experience.

As the months went by, I would find myself waking in the early morning before dawn, Baba immediately in my mind. I would spend several hours, blissful in his company, listening to his words. Then, on the days I did not work, I would sit for sadhana, my mind lost in Baba's presence and bliss until noon. I only knew the passage of time because my body would become exhausted, and he would become practical. He would order me to attend to my body or to my worldly duties.

I find he still assists me with even the place and the time of my sadhana. He comes to me and leaves so as to fit my times with him in with my worldly life. Many times, I would not even know that I needed to attend to the external world, but he would insist, and I would find there was a practical reason. That he does this has always meant a great deal to me. I feel the completeness of his caring in that he bothers to aid me even in these worldly details.

In one such instance that I recall, he came before dawn, waking me from sleep. I was lost in his presence when he suddenly began to insist that I get up. I could not understand this, as it still appeared to be early, and everyone was asleep. I was filled with light and divine bliss and did not want to end my sadhana, but he insisted, so I got up, only to discover that my alarm had not gone off. We had all overslept, and my ride to work would be arriving in ten minutes.

Sadhana on Panther Meadows

One day during this time in my journey, Liam and I decided to take a trip to Mt Shasta to camp on the upper Panther Meadow. While I was camping, I took the opportunity to meditate at the top of the sacred spring. The purest water you could ever imagine bubbles out of the ground and flows from this spring down the meadow amid wildflowers and alpine peaks. The spring has been sacred to the Indians for centuries.

Anyway, I did a long meditation in that power spot that day in the summer of 1989, and in my meditation, I came to Baba in a deep, happy mood of love and spontaneously asked, "How can I serve you?" In my meditation, Baba answered, saying, "Take my hand." My sadhana was very clear. Baba's form, piercing eyes, and vibration were strong. I took his hand in mine. He said, "Place my hand on your heart." I did so, covering it with both of mine in a feeling of love. Then he said that I was to repeat after him. "I swear to serve Guru as Mother to his spiritual children. I vow to give up all personal interest in this service. I swear this before Guru." I repeated this, phrase by phrase, after him. Baba said afterward that this was a serious vow he took from me. He told me I should realize the seriousness of it.

Lahiri Mahasaya's Message

Shortly after my Mt. Shasta experience, during a deep meditation, Lahiri Mahasaya appeared clearly in my mind. He exuded divine joy. His joy was so intoxicating that I could barely refrain from external laughter. He looked at me with this joy, and somehow, I felt as if this joy was directed towards me. It was not exactly personal but an unreserved exquisite joy in the nature of human existence and unfoldment. I can't quite put it into words.

In my sadhana, I went to bow to him; over the years, he has helped me from time to time, but still emanating undaunted joy, he stopped me. He then waved behind him to Baba, who was giving the namaskar mudra, hands folded in prayer. Baba appeared like Krishna, with a thousand multiple images moving outward from both sides behind him. I knew Lahiri Mahasaya was indicating that it is only to Baba I should bow, that my fate is entrusted to him alone. To Baba, I bowed down.

Meditation on the Infinite

A Duty

In September and October, my Baba continued to manifest in the aspect of spiritual husband, his presence filling my mind with effulgent light and unconditioned love. He told me that this infinite presence is the nature of his being.

Then several weeks before his physical departure, in early October, he said, "My consciousness will grow within you now and bear fruit. You are spiritual wife to me, carrying within you my essential nature in seed form." During these weeks, Baba was very close, spending long hours with me in subtle form, the room thick with his beautiful scent and his aura. I felt that my heart had melted open.

In the last few weeks before Baba's passing, he also began to talk to me about duty. He said to me, "As *Guru Deva*, I give you a duty." In twenty years, my inner Baba had never referred to himself as "Guru Deva" or talked to me about duty. He had never asked anything of me. This was new. He said, "I give you the duty of service to me. This is your only duty. To love me and to serve me. I give each a duty according to their disposition. As your bent is solely towards me, so I give you this duty."

This, of course, delighted my heart, but then I would think, "How can this be real? Baba, I understand this in meditation, but on the physical plane, I am not near you or part of your inner circle; furthermore, I am a woman. How can this be my duty?" He would never answer this inquiry.

Very frequently, during these first few weeks in October, he would ask me, "What is your duty?" and have me repeat it to him. Still confused about this duty, I finally asked him, "Baba, I know that you care for all living beings. Why don't you give me a duty that is serving humanity?" He said to me, "The greatest service you can give to humanity is to focus on the Supreme. This is humanity's greatest need. Be one with the Supreme, and the service is automatic."

Longing to See My Physical Guru

A deep source of unhappiness for me over the years has been my lack of contact with my physical guru, Shrii Shrii Anandamurti. I was busy raising my family, and he was far away in India. There was one opportunity that arose in 1989 when Anandamurti Baba scheduled a trip to see Western devotees in Jamaica. I wanted to go to see him, but I was reluctant to travel, and my Baba discouraged me. Then mentally, he held me close in his presence while I cried for days that I could not go to be near the guru's physical manifestation.

It feels as if there has been an invisible barrier over the years preventing me from returning to him as a physical guru. For some time in the spring of 1990, my inner Baba indicated a desire to come to America in the physical form of Guru. He asked that I and others send him invitations, but something shifted before I could do so. He said nothing, but he no longer wished for an invitation. I could feel in him that something had changed. He would not be coming. It was too late. I knew he would be leaving this world instead, but I did not know when.

During the last year of his life, I wanted to see my physical guru. But I could not go without Baba's internal permission, and this I could not get. He put me off. He said it would not work to see me in India. This led me to hope and dream that Baba might come here, and I might see him. He would tell me, "To know the *Satguru* is a rare and great gift. To be in his physical presence is a great blessing, but that, when it can be done, it is even better to know him internally." He said he would cultivate internal dependence in me, not external reliance.

It is true that when I was with him as a physical guru, I was extremely attached to him. Then he was in prison, the years passed, and the invisible barrier arose. All he would have had to do as an inner guru was to say to come to him. But instead, this year, to my inquiries, he was reluctant, putting me off and denying permission for me to go to India.

In the last months before his departure, I felt a real need to see the guru in his physical form. To my inquiries, he would say that the feeling was mutual. He desired to see me also, but he could not see me in India. He would show me a room, which, when I later went to India, I discovered was the darshan hall in his quarters in Calcutta. In the vision, he would be surrounded by orange-robed monks and nuns, and I would be far away, lost in the crowd. I would feel hurt by this vision of distance and would cry in response. He would then say, "To be a mere face in the crowd would break your tender heart; you are too close to me, and I cannot bring you near me." In this way, he refused me until the news of his physical death.

Knowing Baba's Departure

In the months before Baba's leaving, I felt concerned for his physical health. In my sadhana, I begged him to leave India and care for his health. But I was deflected with vague promises that he would see me again. During the summer, I had difficult dreams that I could never get to where he was, and when I got there, he had just left. I dreamed that he was in danger.

In September of 1990, about a month before Baba's departure, during one meditation, I felt around the edges of his being that his physical death was imminent. My mind became rebellious, and I began to think, "Even without his permission, I must go immediately to see him. The time is very short." But again, when I requested to see him, he deflected me. He said, "It is true you should see me one more time, but wait a little longer, then you can come."

Thus, I knew I would be going to India shortly, but I assumed he meant before his departure, so I was surprised to find out the news when it came. It was clear to me that Anandamurti Baba knew of his departure at this time and, I believe, had known about it since late spring to early summer. But my assumption that he meant he would see me before his physical death proved wrong.

The night of his death, there was no warning for me. In the morning, just before the call came, I was with Baba in meditation, in a blissful mood. He asked me my duty again and had me repeat it to him. To my inquiries about how this could be my duty, there was only mental silence.

He would not address it. He did not warn me. The fateful phone call from another devotee was like a dream that I had lived in fear of for many months. I had imagined this call from her over and over in my mind. When it actually happened, it felt like walking through a dream, enacting what had already occurred in my mind's eye.

I immediately went back to my Baba, who was patiently unshaken. He simply said, "I have opened your heart, and now I will break it, and in the crack, real divinity will bloom." He said to me, "I am always with you. I will always be with you. You have lost nothing but an unfulfilled desire (for his physical darshan) that you will have to give up."

I knew he would always be with me, but my heart was broken regardless. I would never have his physical touch, never be able to touch his feet, to sit in his presence physically. To remain alive without him physically on the planet, I didn't know if I wanted to, or could bear to. Even though I had not seen the physical guru in years, the loss was excruciating. I knew that I, of all people, had lost nothing. I had not been with him physically for eighteen years. Everything had come to me from the inner level. But I still felt the loss of the closest person in the world to me, as though I had lost my reason for being here.

In Sadhana, the evening after I heard of Baba's leaving, I sent my mind to him in India. I saw that Baba was laid out in a room with people around him. His body had a special glow and was very cold. In his subtle body, he sat beside his physical body, and joy emanated from him.

He threw flowers to everyone as they sat with their eyes closed in deep meditation. I understood this as a shower of blessings. I was happy to know of his joy at this event, that no sorrow was in him. I was glad for him, though pained in myself.

Chapter IX
Return to India

*T*wenty years ago, when my Baba first came to me, my inner life of meditation suddenly and dramatically opened, turning my life upside down with unusual experiences. This opening led to the feet of Shrii Shrii Anandamurti as my physical guru. I had hoped that now, as my sadhana had again accelerated, I might be able to turn to him as a physical guru for guidance and help. How could this critical time for me coincide with his leaving? It was too painful. So, I cried, and the overpowering feeling came that I must go to India. When I went to the inner guru, he said, "I request your presence near to me at this time. You may come."

Going to India, Again

This was apparently what he meant when he said he would see me one more time. But to go to India without my family, my husband and children, was very adventuresome for me. I had not traveled alone in years. I began to be afraid of the journey, fearful of being far away from home. But my Baba sweetly insisted, "You must come." To my surprise, the material plane obstacles, such as no passport, dissipated with ease. Other devotees of Baba were there as traveling companions. All was going well, but I still felt fear.

The night before I was to leave, the fear became extreme, opening like a pit of terror. I told my husband I was too afraid to go, but I knew Baba wanted me to. I called to Baba, saying, "If you want me to go, please help me. The fear is too strong." I went to bed, my mind in turmoil. Finally, after much tossing and turning, I was able to fall asleep for a few hours.

Then in the early morning, when it was still dark, my Baba woke me with extreme sweetness and caring. He kindly said, "Not to worry," and told me he would protect me for my entire journey. He spoke sweetly to me, saying, "I will surround you with family to ensure you are not alone, and I will personally be with you, ensuring your comfort and safety. I request your presence at this time. Now you may come."

As Baba had promised, my trip to India was safe and easy. My deep-seated fear dissolved when I got to the airport and never returned. My friends knew what to do, and they took care of everything. I felt loved and protected the entire journey. Grief was my only discomfort.

Upon arriving in Calcutta, India, we went straight to the ashram compound. I felt the strong emanations of Baba's aura begin to affect me from the moment I entered the ashram. It was a walled compound with several buildings inside. I looked around as I walked in, immediately overcome by the confusion surrounding me. There were guards in gray standing near entrances, clutching large sticks; orange-robed monks and nuns going this way and that; and crowds of Indian devotees everywhere. Yet amid the chaos flowed the sweet waves of Baba's blissful presence that filled the space.

Saying Goodbye

I found my quarters, then went as soon as possible to view Baba's body. As I approached the room where Baba's body lay, his vibration became increasingly dominant. There was a line of people waiting to enter. It was hot, and people's faces were shiny with sweat. Women in saris, some with small children, Indian men in white shirts called kurtas, the push of bodies one against another, and the scent of incense combined with the musk of closely pressed people greeted me in the line. I stood behind a family. People were crying. Some sobbed violently. Orange-robed men and women kept the line moving in and out of the room.

I was ushered into the room by an orange-robed nun, a *sannyasin*. As I entered the small adobe chamber, I saw Baba's body laid out on a platform against a white silk background with ice (to preserve it) and flowers surrounding him. People ahead of me were moving through, some sobbing and wailing, not wanting to leave, being pulled away by the monks and nuns. I looked at Baba and felt a wave of divine energy overpower me. Around his body, the attraction to his manifestation was agonizingly intense. There was love and bliss in that moment. Yet the pain of being denied his physical presence for so long also arose, like a knife in my heart; the experience of seeing him was bittersweet. An orange-robed nun laid her hand on my shoulder, letting me know I needed to leave. I turned away and moved to the exit as if in a dream.

I spent most of the evening going through the room where he was laid out, again and again, and then doing meditation, integrating the internal presence and the external guru. At some point, my inner Baba got annoyed with me and said I must do something to care for my physical body. I got up and began to leave, but seeing people entering again, I was drawn to follow them. My Baba's voice boomed in my mind, saying, "No! I forbid it!"

There was no going against that, so I left to care for my body as he wanted. It really was in extreme lack of both food and sleep. I went to the women's quarters—a tall, multi-storied concrete building in one corner of the ashram compound, to sleep—and to my surprise, the nuns were preparing food. I had a solid meal, thanks to their kindness and help. After the meal, it was late. I took off my sari and was opening my sleeping bag, preparing for bed, when I heard the loudspeaker announcing, *"Anandamurti Arati...,"* a kind of prayer.

A deep, overpowering urge came over me to be near Baba's form. I knew I could not stay away on his last night. Without even thinking to put on my sari, just dressed in a simple skirt and blouse, I grabbed my shawl and ran to the compound where Baba's body was laid out. It was late, maybe twelve or one, and it seemed hundreds of people were going the other way, returning to their quarters for the night.

It didn't make sense to be running over there at this late hour. I had no idea what I would find, but the feeling inside was compelling. When I entered the compound, I found it filled with people, many sleeping on the ground near the wall. I thought, "All these Indian devotees are sleeping here. I will find a bit of wall to lean on and spend the night here near my Lord." But I couldn't find any wall. Every inch was taken.

A line of people was still going into Baba's quarters in small groups. Only Indian men were there, so I felt awkward, but I stood with them regardless, drawn by an overpowering feeling. This time the groups of people were moving slowly through the room. There was more time to be near Baba's form. The waves of divine love near his body were potent. When I left the room, he said in my mind, "Stay near to me." I could not leave his proximity, so I sat down outside the room. However, I was no one in the large community around Baba and had no privileges. Very few people even knew me. I thought I might be forced to leave, but no one bothered me.

When I sat down, my mind went into Baba's room, straight to him. The feeling of him became overwhelming. There was only the white effulgence of his aura. In my mind, I said to him, as I had been saying all day in meditation, "My Lord, now that you are not in this world, I have no further use for this body. You are losing that form. You give it in profound sacrifice and love for living beings. If you have any need for this one, it is yours. If it is your desire, I will step aside for you. What I have is yours, if you wish, in any way you wish."

To my outpouring of feelings, he answered, "Yes. I accept your offering." My mind then slipped into a deep effulgence. No thought could enter or rise. Though there was awareness of occasional external sounds, the mind did not react. No thought, no concentration, no "I" to concentrate. Baba, ideation, and the one who ideates effortlessly lost distinction. This person was gone. There was only effulgence. There was a body. There was a mind. But where there had been a person, there was no one; no Baba, no me, only effulgence.

When I arose from my sadhana, it was morning. In those predawn hours, I felt I could not leave his proximity; the bond was too strong. Despite three days of little or no sleep, I knew I should stay awake. The greatness of his love required that I honor him by bearing witness to this process, maintaining a vigil until the process was completed and his body gone. It was my small sacrifice to endure some physical hardship in honor of him. It felt right.

They asked us to leave while they cleaned the area. I went to the bottom of Baba's compound. A memory from the previous night arose unbidden in my mind. I recalled hearing someone saying, "Trance (absorption in divine rapture) and of all nights this one, perhaps this has import." In response to this recollection, Baba's voice came into my mind, saying, "Face it." I knew he meant I should face the import of my experiences the last few months, including this night. He was letting me know that it had significance, but my mind reeled from this line of thought. I would not go down that road, despite his command. I did not want to face what my Baba had been saying to me internally since before his departure. I did not want to think there was an import to my experience.

Instead, I went to look at Baba's Garden, which I knew he loved, to see what he enjoyed in this life and to be happy in his enjoyment. It was as if I could feel the things he loved. I felt inside that he wanted to show me the things he loved in his worldly life, that I might appreciate them and know them just because they were a part of him. I felt as if I knew him so well, though really, it had been so many years since I had known him as a physical person. I felt as if I knew him from the inside looking out, rather than through an outside encounter. I felt as if I knew what he would love, what he would approve of, and his feelings about things, as if they were a part of me. It was a sweet feeling.

I went back as soon as I could, to sit outside the room where his body lay, to do my personal vigil in honor of him. I could not meditate deeply as my body was far beyond its limits. Some people were crying hard and strongly reacting to their final viewing of Baba's body. I felt great beauty in their pain, the sincerity of their need, and the incredible beauty of the human heart. I wanted to comfort them. I was touched by the depth of the gift Baba had given to so many, stirring the core of their hearts in yearning for the Supreme. Their human beauty, their longing, the agony of their loss, and their greatness hung together, bittersweet.

I went through the viewing line again quickly, and then we were asked to leave. I did not feel right leaving, as I heard Baba's soft request in my mind, "Stay near to me." An orange-robed nun approached me and tried to pull me away from outside the room where Baba's body lay. The nun was saying, "Come, you have to go." An overpowering feeling remained in me that I wasn't this girl from the United States. I was a deeper person who was a part of Baba's immediate family, a family of lifetimes. I told her, "Don't interfere with what you don't understand," as I knew something was happening that no one around me understood. And, in fact, I, as a conscious person, did not understand—but this deeper person within me understood it perfectly well.

Four or five times in my life, this same deeper persona has come to the surface. It feels like an old and conscious soul that is a conglomerate of all my lives, one who has lived long enough to be fairly awake, not a soul asleep from life to life. As we go from life to life, perhaps we are aware—when we come out of our body—of all our conglomerate experiences. But when we enter another physical body, we forget who we are and then spend our lives trying to figure it out.

This person seems to have done that enough times not to be entirely unconscious. Male and a close family member to Baba, this persona—this deeper sense of self—felt a duty to keep this vigil for Baba. Perhaps this part of me is also where the sense of a destiny I had as a child comes from. I was in an altered state and did not understand these feelings, but I knew, at that time with

Baba, that I had a duty from the past I needed to fulfill.

When the cremation started, it was time to go and sit in the crowd. I left the compound and went in to find a seat. I silently watched the flames. I saw the birds circling overhead. When the heat became excessive, and I began to feel ill from it, I noticed how the clouds came in to shelter us from the sun. I watched for hours until it was over, and my Lord's physical person passed from this world. When only ashes remained, friends brought me to a hotel, where I found food and rest.

Guru Shakti

The next day, Baba woke me from sleep in the early morning before dawn. As I awoke, I smelled the sweet, dry scents of India wafting in from the open window. Memory returned of the plain but clean hotel room I had entered in a fog of exhaustion the prior night. It was still dark outside, the air was pleasantly warm, and an overhead fan gently turned in preparation for the hot day ahead.

As Baba's presence flowed fully into my awareness, he said gently, "I have infused your being with my Guru Shakti. The essence of my consciousness now lives within you in seed form." He then requested that I return to the ashram and tell his sons, the monks in charge of the community, what he had done. He told me I should be candid and open with them. He said this would be difficult for me but that he must think of the welfare of others as well. He said they needed to know what he had done.

Suddenly I was fully awake, my mind rebelling from these instructions. To start with, I had never heard the term, Guru Shakti. Although I had a general idea from what he said, I wasn't entirely sure what it meant. What on earth was he talking about? How could I possibly tell these monks, who had been with Baba for years and whom I didn't know, my inner experience?

Deeply disturbed, I said to Baba, "This can't be. This cannot possibly be true. I'm not enlightened." He replied, "It is never done that way. It is not an enlightened mind that this must be passed to, but a properly prepared mind with the proper *samskaras* or mental tendencies. Your Shakti is active now. Mine remains in seed form so that proper adjustments can be made. Yours is a fertile mind in which this seed will grow and bear fruit. This seed remains dormant now. Soon it will stir and begin to grow."

Giving further explanation, Baba said, "What I have done is not the passage of a lineage but the merging of subtle layers of the mind, a kind of melding of minds and hearts. That is why I call it a spiritual marriage, a marriage of subtle levels. You are still an individual, an evolving being with a small sense of self. Yet you hold within you the seed of my consciousness. Rather than a lineage, this is a marriage of mind and spirit."

Still distressed, I mentally declared, "This can *not* be true! Baba leaves his connection with everyone!"

Baba calmly replied, "This is true, but not my Shakti." He then told me once again that his Guru Shakti could only be left in a properly prepared mind with proper mental tendencies. He reaffirmed that, as hard as it would be for me, I must let his sons know, for their benefit.

I got up, completely shaken by his words. I soon became convinced that I had gone off the deep end. There was no proof that any of this was real. Two days remained before I was scheduled to leave. Baba requested that I do this before I leave India. I could not. My mind raged between wanting to do what my Baba needed me to and my fear that this was all a delusion. He had never demanded I do anything before, and just the prior night, I had sincerely offered everything I had to him without qualification. Now, the first thing he asked of me, I couldn't do it. My mind was reeling. And so began my extreme mental clash.

Later in the day, I took a rickshaw through the busy streets of Calcutta to the ashram compound. Despite the pressure I felt in my mind, I could not talk to anyone. I thought, "These people were very close to the physical guru. They have dedicated their lives to him. I am a stranger. This can't be true. I can't intrude upon their grief with my insanity." Then again, I would wonder, "What if it were true, and I am disobeying my beloved Baba's request?" That thought was equally agonizing.

I wandered aimlessly through the ashram, lost in my internal struggle, until I saw an American man I knew from the States. We said hi, and I summoned the courage and asked if we could talk. We walked over to a quiet spot with some chairs, and I proceeded to tell him about my experience. He listened carefully but was noncommittal in response. I felt like a complete fool even talking to this man I already knew, much less to the monks in charge. So, I meditated and attended some programs but could not bring myself to act.

The next morning, my final day in India, I resolved to write what Baba had said in a letter and send it to the community's General Secretary, despite my fears. I wrote the letter with Baba's loving encouragement but couldn't bring it forward. During that day, I felt an intense strain on my mind, as if Baba applied mental force on the one hand and my resistance applied pressure on the other. I

Chapter X
The Dark Night of Grief and Doubt

Beloved of my heart,
The vision of you is as sweet as the honey of your words.
When you are near, your scent fills the air.

Love is boundless.

To be near to you is to feel the joy of union.
To feel the mingling, the blending
Of your Self and my small self
Is your gracious gift.

You are the life of my life, The heart of my heart.
My eyes are only to behold your brightness.
My ears only to hear your call.

When you are near, all forms become your form.
When you are near, sweetness prevails.
But my Lord, when you are afar,
I cannot bear this life.

When I awake, my pillow is wet with tears,
For I have cried for you in my sleep.
My eyes are wet, and tears stream
Endlessly down my cheeks.

Your dream is in my mind.
But in the dream, you are gone.
And I long for you.

Longing consumes me.
Where have you gone, Guru of my heart?
How is it that your form no longer walks this dusty earth?
How is it I remain when you are not with me?

My heart is awash with love and sorrow.
I know no end to this pain.
I know no way to stop the tears.
No cure for love.

I had been away in India for only a few short weeks, but the experience changed my life. The sublime, blissful spiritual opening I had been experiencing for over a year shifted during this time to deep grief and internal conflict about Guru Shakti.

My inner process consumed me, yet it had to give way to the needs of my sons, now four and eleven, my husband, and my work. Upon my return from India, I needed to resume my worldly duties. So, I settled into daily life with my family and returned to work as a psychologist. I did what was expected of me, but whenever I had a moment to be alone, I struggled with the grief and conflict within me.

Grief

Baba's physical departure was a huge loss, as if something inside me was gone. There was a vacant place where his physical presence had been. Even though his spiritual presence was with me, there was still this feeling of profound loss. All I could do was cry. In the months that followed my return and his departure, tears streamed endlessly from my eyes. I had lost my grandmother, mother, father, and animals I loved. Grief was no stranger to me, yet I had never experienced such pain of loss.

Baba, on the inner plane, would be with me throughout the night, my mind drifting between my dream of him and his soft words gently comforting me. Yet sometimes in the morning, I would feel wetness on my face and realize I had been crying in my sleep.

I had returned from India to my existing job at the Developmental Center, a hundred-year-old state institution that was previously a psychiatric hospital. It had become a locked facility for people with intellectual disabilities. During the months after my return, I would appear to be okay when I was with people. While working as a psychologist, I would enter the facility using my key, going through the locked doors into my office each day. I would then go down into the unit, or ward as they used to be called in the old days, unlock the door, and step inside.

My first thought upon entering would be to locate staff and clients and look for dangerous situations. My clients were the most violent in the Developmental Center. The danger posed by walking on the unit could not be taken lightly. It was part of my job, and I was skilled at keeping myself safe. I would see my clients and talk with them as best I could, ask staff some relevant questions, and return to my office. But after I entered my office and closed the door behind me, I would break down crying, overcome with grief. I would write my reports, tears in my eyes. Then, after some time, I would dry my eyes, go out again, and be with my clients or colleagues.

As time went on, my conflict and grief continued to distress me. So, one day at work, I asked a close colleague, a psychologist, if we could talk. I openly told her what had happened to me in India and the experiences I was having. I thought she would reject the authenticity of my story, but instead, she told me that she did not doubt that my inner experiences were completely real. This colleague was a strong Roman Catholic, and she had had some near-death experiences and profound mystical visions herself, so she understood. She did not doubt mine—but I did. Yet her acceptance gave me pause.

My husband and the few close friends I confided in also understood and supported me in my profound grief and the Guru Shakti experience. I was getting support from friends and colleagues whom I'd told what had happened, though I myself remained skeptical.

The deep, overwhelming grief was mixed with an incredible challenge to my reality. It was not just grief. The strain of the transition that was going on informed my experience. It was something coming from the unconscious that was more than I could rationally understand or put together.

Life went on thus, working, being with family and friends, then grieving and stressing. December came and went. Christmas, a favorite time of year, came and went. I had trouble getting into Christmas and putting out energy. I didn't care. I went through the motions, but I was only half present. At work, I went through the motions as well.

Dreams

When there were dreams, they would be about Baba being gone, aspects of his departure, or guidance for me. In one dream that stayed with me, Baba was standing around with his lawyers. They were his monks and people I did not know. In the dream, he was preparing for his departure by distributing his estates or assigning different tasks to various people.

I stood to one side as he walked to different monks or lawyers and assigned aspects of what needed to happen. After talking to several other people, he came over to where I was standing and told me he wanted me to do a portion of the work that he was leaving. Then in the dream, he gave me a hug. When he hugged me, light and love were everywhere. I don't remember the rest of the dream.

There were many dreams—a *lot* of dreams. They were a continual nightly experience. In another dream, I went into Baba's room. The energy was high and blissful, but he was leaving. I wanted to go with him, but he said, "No. You can't come yet. You must stay here. You still have work to do." I was sad. I couldn't go with him. I just wanted to merge into him, meld into him. I wanted to go, but it wasn't time yet. He said I had to stay.

In another dream of Baba leaving, many orange-robed monks and nuns were sitting down to help Baba. I came in, bringing a group of people with me. Baba was lying on a bed, and the people were in a waiting area below. One nun was helping Baba pull up the covers. I came and helped tuck him into bed and prepare to see people, but he was sick and was going to leave. Many of the dreams were like this; Baba was leaving. Then in other dreams, he would comfort me, give me instructions, and tell me about what was happening to me. He would reassure me in the dreams regarding his leaving, saying not to worry; he was still with me. In the dreams, he would tell me that what he was saying to me was going to happen. It was not my imagination.

Vision Sleep

After a few months of nightly dreams, this nighttime experience deepened. Several months went by when I did not sleep at all. Instead of sleep, every night, I would go into a subtly altered state of consciousness in which Baba's presence would fill my psyche, giving teachings and being with me in a state of infinite, divine love. I would remain in this altered state the entire night. Grieving and conflict flowed through me, as well as blissful states where I would feel that everything is one consciousness, only one existence.

This subtle state of being was deeply comforting, and despite not sleeping, I felt rested in the mornings. I would rise, meditate, see my family, and go to work at the Developmental Center. After work, I would come home and take care of my children, meditate, and go into these different states. Somehow, I maintained my life through it all. The only relief from my grief and longing to be near Baba would come when the boundaries would thin in these altered states, and I could feel deeply close to Baba.

Despite my experiences and Baba's efforts, I could not accept what he said about Guru Shakti and thus felt torn between love and doubt.

Mt. Shasta

That summer, my family and I went on a camping trip to Mt. Shasta. This was our family tradition. As I mentioned earlier, Liam and I had spent many summers on the mountain, meditating in Shasta's legendary high mountain vibration. It was our little Himalayas of the West. When our kids came along, we kept up the tradition, at least for a week or two each year, but included them and their interests. We set up camp in a cozy campground partway up the mountain, with great views of the peak.

As soon as we were set up and Liam was looking after the kids, I took my journal and copies of the *Bhagavad*

Gita and the *Yoga Sutras* and went just outside the campground to a private area under a tree, next to a brook. The spot was about ten feet from where the water naturally gushed out of the earth in a sacred spring. I began reading. The teachings, combined with the high spiritual energy of the place, sent my mind into a state of bliss, mingled with my continued grief about Shrii Shrii Anandamurti's physical departure. I wavered between joy and grief in bittersweet moments.

I wrote for a time in my journal and fell deeper into communion with all that is. Baba's presence then came. It felt as if every molecule was his form—every leaf, every branch, the sky, the mountain, the water in the brook, the earth itself—everything was his form. My Beloved was embodied everywhere, in all forms. I basked in this profound and exquisite communion for an undefined passage of time.

When I arose from my meditation, I went with joy to play with my children and feel the love of the Infinite all around me—in the mountains, in the sunshine, and in my family. This meditative experience of unity continued during my stay on the mountain.

One evening I was alone in our tent, reading and talking to Baba, when grief welled up. The feeling arose that I could choose to leave my body and that if I did, I would die. I felt I had no reason to go on with Baba gone. Even though I had my family, career, and life, I felt, with Baba physically gone, as if I had lost my purpose for being here. Responding to these thoughts, Baba said, "I want you to stay for at least twenty years to do this work for me." He was referring to the expression of his consciousness that he had been talking to me about. He said that this was my reason to be here now and that I needed to stay.

I sat in my tent, realizing this was a pivotal moment on Mt. Shasta. I was deep enough into the grieving process that I felt I could leave. I felt I was at a pivotal point. I could leave. I knew this to be true. I knew it with a great deal of certainty. Yet I needed to stay. Baba was directing me to stay. At that moment, I chose life and, on some deep level, to do the work Baba was asking of me. I chose to meet the loss and pain head-on and to try to find my way through to him again, here in this life.

The grief, longing, love, and heartache of this time are hard to put into words and perhaps are best expressed in the poetry of my heart.

My Beloved, I feel as arid
As a dusty desert swept by a dry wind
As empty as a hollow promise
Dreamed but never fulfilled.

I would cry, but there are no tears in me.
I am numb. I cannot even define my pain,
Only you are not near.

I do not feel the sweetness of your breath,
Or the loveliness of your touch.
I am alone.

I cannot soar on wings
Into the hearts and minds of all beings.
I do not fly with the eagle.
I am not still in the ancient wood.

I cannot span the stars,
Nor can I touch the inner heart.
There is only the wasteland
Of my separateness.

How can I find You?
I cannot even call your name.

My mind weaves sweet memories of you,
But what would make you come again,
And stay with me?

I have no wealth to barter.
No greatness to attract you.
No impressive discipline to allow me to
Demand from you.

I have no power over you.
My mind is too simple to know
What to do or not to do
To capture You.

So, I will sit by the door of our house,
And wait for you, my Beloved.
And I will dream of memories,
When You were near.

When I could touch nothing but you,
When all forms were your form.
And in your embrace
Heaven and earth became one.

I will dream and dream,
Until perhaps someday
I will look up from where I sit dreaming,
And You will stand before me,
My Beloved

Doubt

During the same period of time in which I was grieving, I was also struggling with Baba's guidance about Guru Shakti and all it implied. In my grief and despair, I concluded that my inner guidance about Guru Shakti must be madness, that somehow my Baba was misleading me. I thought I had lost my guru and perhaps my sanity. I could not face what had happened.

The Allegories

When I had time to be alone, my Baba began to explain that my inability to act in India was due to judging my experience with my limited understanding, rather than with faith in his knowledge. Frankly confronting me, he said my concern for the monks' opinions of me was stronger than my concern for their welfare and that this made me unable to follow his instructions. I could not refute what he was saying, as my limitation was apparent.

During the following months, a series of allegories unfolded in my internal dialogue. Allegory can be a medium for the spirit to talk to the psyche, often speaking in images and symbols that the soul and the heart understand, even if the mind cannot. Through these, Baba opened my psyche to the transformation I was going through.

The allegory of a mantle emerged, with Baba telling me that he was passing his mantle to me. He noted that this mantle was weighty and would crush all small aspects of myself because the welfare of many souls rests on it and that it requires service and personal sacrifice. "It will change you. This mantle is one of devotion to the welfare of suffering humanity. It will require the full utilization of my Gift. I am Guru. I have given you the Gift of direct experience. It is a very great boon. You must wear this mantle. Your direct experience will guide others. I have said I will lead through you. I mean this. You think, "I am small. I can never hold such a weight." I say, "I am strong—and I will hold it for you in your form.""

"You have nothing to fear. I will help. I shall make your path free to express what is within. I have placed my mantle; its weight will do the rest. You think you are inadequate, but you are not a proper judge. Your objectivity is lacking. I am a very good judge. You must trust my judgment."

When I would go deep in meditation, I would see images, or my inner guide would communicate to me with deepest love—saying, "Be as Parvati to Shiva; convey my guidance; be mother to my children; the flame, the seed..." In the dance of Baba's teachings, these symbolic images kept arising.

In another meditation, the image of a vessel arose as Baba related, "You are a vessel for the Divine to express his affection, his love. "A vessel need not be beautiful. It need not be holy. It is only a holder. It is that which resides within the vessel which is of importance. Be a vessel so that others may drink of my essence from this cup."

Again, in a deep meditation, Baba requested that I come close to him. In the inner realm, I went to my guru within and, expressing my heart, said that my only desire was to serve. My inner guide responded, "A devotee can have no desire but the Lord's desire. This is personal service to Guru, to give his love and serve his desire that all beings should have the opportunity to return to the Infinite One."

The allegories continued to unfold in my meditations during this time. Baba commented to me in meditation, saying he had lit the flame of my heart with the flame of his heart and that I would light the flame of others from the flame of my heart. In this way, it is passed onwards, and the flame is kept eternal: the eternal flame. As he spoke, I saw my Lord's flame in my mind's eye, bright behind me, and then the flame of my heart. In front of me, I saw the flames of many people's hearts. I asked, "Baba, is this your desire?" He responded, "Yes, my child, it is. This is my work, and as my servant, it becomes yours."

When I would be in a more worldly state of mind, not dominated by my heart, I could not understand why I was having these experiences. Yet try as I might, I could not escape them. These themes would come when I would surrender to the Divine in meditation.

During this phase of transformation, I was still going back and forth mentally. I would sometimes get into my delusion theory and begin to feel that reality. I would think, "No, no, no. This is pushing the envelope here. This is just a little bit much; this kind of experience cannot be happening to me!" Then Baba would come and talk to me, be comforting, reassure me, and I would again be convinced that my experience was real. Thus, I went back and forth in my thinking for months, confused and distressed.

Transformation

As I reflect upon this time in my journey of the soul, I cannot help but comment on the nature of transformation. If the spiritual path were an easy walk, surely many more would seek its benefits. However, opening to the full nature of our divine essence requires us to face our inner demons and look at our shadow side with complete honesty and self-disclosure. Lacking this, our self-limiting beliefs and behaviors keep us from truly diving deep into our human potential to the Divinity within.

Yet when confronted with our core issues, we tend to evade, deny, and do whatever we can to maintain our status quo. True transformation requires not simply moving the pieces around inside our psyches but actually changing levels of consciousness. This type of fundamental change can be challenging, and this type of personal work is often difficult—yet necessary in order to have the soul-baring authenticity needed to meet the Divine within.

Herein comes the role of Guru, the one who leads from darkness to light, who helps us cross barriers we could not face on our own. I have said before that the only true guru is Brahma or God, the Infinite. That One can manifest in congenial forms, both outer and inner, to communicate with our human psyche. It has manifested for me in the form of my Baba and the teachings he has given in his dance with me—teachings that, though sometimes difficult, I feel have brought true transformation in my psyche.

The experience of the loss of Baba's physical presence and his inner guidance to me was difficult to accept because it brought my inner world and my outer life into collision with each other. I had always kept my sense of destiny and the inner experiences of Baba very private. I was unsure if they would be socially acceptable or easily understood by others, and it was easier not to mention them. I had built a successful life for myself, both with family and friends and professionally, but my inner and outer worlds were not integrated.

With this guidance from Baba, I was asked to act in the external world based on my internal experiences. This crossed the line of my comfort zone and caused a tremendous crisis within me. On the persona ego level, I could not understand why I was having such a high level of grief over someone I hadn't been around for eighteen years, and I could not accept that this passing of the flame, or Guru Shakti experience, would happen to me.

Yet in the deeper thread of my existence, where my feelings of destiny and passionate love for the Divine had been lying since early childhood, I wanted proximity to Baba. In the depths of meditation, it all made sense. I believed Baba. This deeper aspect of me felt that the closest being to me in the world had just left his physical body. I think the grief hit me so hard because, inside, I felt I had come to this planet for Baba. In this deeper aspect, there was a strong sense that my feeling of destiny was a commitment from the past, from before this life. This part of me knew my destiny.

The challenge posed by these two sides of myself coming together was creating a kind of war inside of me. My rational mind was having trouble grappling with it all, putting it all in one package that made sense. The conflict was high. And in addition, the lifelong inhibition about bringing the deeper person within to the surface of my existence was ingrained in me, making what Baba was saying paralyzing.

It didn't make sense to me when he said to give his guidance. I had never given spiritual direction to anybody. I had never received any advice from Baba for any other person. I had only personal guidance from my Baba. My inhibition was not about what others might think of me or that they might judge me to be crazy, as much as that I thought I was so inadequate. I have had fears and emotional issues. I thought I was not qualified to have this type of experience.

Denial

The winter passed, and spring came and went. I was still in my internal process. By late spring of 1991, I had convinced myself that everything Baba had told me was a lie and that none of this was real. I began to come out of the grieving process. Yet, simultaneously, my internal re-action to the idea of some special transmission of Guru's spiritual energy had reached an intolerable level.

I just wanted to live a normal life. I could not wrap my head around this being real. There was still no out-ward indication that any of what I experienced in India about Guru Shakti or what my Baba had said before or since had any external validity. And as time passed, it began to feel even more like some dream or delusion. I just wanted to put it all behind me.

After almost eight months of this inner conflict—and of questioning my sanity—I was done. I concluded that I had suffered a mental breakdown due to the extreme stress of my guru's passing and of being in India. My Baba's continued reassurance of its reality didn't matter. Rational thinking could only conclude that this could not happen to me. I was not part of his inner circle; I wasn't worthy, and this kind of thing just doesn't happen to or-dinary people like me.

I was now clear in my analysis and firm in my deci-sion to reject this crossover from my inner experience of my Baba to this craziness. After concluding that this was all absurd and delusional, I felt I had resolved my inter-nal conflict. That is, until the acute panic attacks started.

Panic and Resolution

Within a few weeks of this decision to reject it all, I began to have terrible panic attacks. They were frequent, happening multiple times a day, and devastating. They would come on out of nowhere. I would suddenly be struck with immobilizing fear, palms sweating, and heart pounding. Unable to think and afraid to be alone, I would hold my husband's hands and try to get through it. I didn't know why they were happening or what to do about it.

I finally called a psychiatrist at a local clinic to seek help. These unbearable panic attacks were ruining my life. I made an appointment with the psychiatrist, and when I saw her, my experience was very different from what had happened with the psychiatrist I saw in my early twenties. This woman really listened, and I openly told her what had happened to me. Much to my shock, she supported the validity of the experiences I had been having! It seemed everybody believed in the reality of my experience except me.

These high anxiety and panic states continued for two to three months before I finally realized I had been running from my sense of destiny. I had been running from my inner relationship with Baba, hoping to resolve my internal conflicts, but it wasn't working. I realized that by rejecting my destiny and my guru, I was setting up a deeper conflict inside of me than the one I feared. It hit me that I could not keep running from myself.

The extreme mental pain caused me to take a serious

look at what I was doing. I realized that not only the bliss but also the pain was from Baba. He had allowed me to walk into it so that I might learn. What I learned is that, in my resistance, I had been following fear instead of love. What I learned is that it doesn't matter what the world thinks or even what I think; all that matters is to follow that Love, which is Guru and is in the core of the heart.

What I learned is that the divine Beloved of my heart means more to me than anything else, and that I needed to let go of trying to control things. I realized I knew nothing. I did not know what was real or unreal, what was right or what was wrong. I did not know if I was adequate or inadequate for the task. What I did know is that divine love and presence are precious—and that to follow my heart, surrender to love, and accept the will and guidance of the Divine is my destiny. I realized that the Beloved of my heart deserves nothing less than absolute surrender.

So, I made a choice. I made a choice to stop fighting my Baba; to stop listening to my concerns, my fears, and my inferiority feelings. I made a choice to follow him, without question, to walk the inner road. I chose to give my life to God, lead it on his terms, and follow the core of my heart and my Beloved who resides there. I realized the way out of fear was to face up to what Baba was telling me, accept my destiny, and surrender my fate into the hands of my Beloved. It would take something I have always been short on—trust and faith in my inner guru and in myself.

Chapter XI
Rising from the Ashes

My cat is in my arms,
I stroke his fur.
Sleepily he looks at me,
Affectionately I hold him near.

His life is neither good nor bad.
He moves through this world,
Accepting joy and sorrow
Patiently living and being a cat.

I feel this simple one,
I see into the core.
I know it is my Lord,
Looking to be a cat with a cat's mind.

Wearing the simplicity of a mind grown from nature
Bearing the body of a cat
He rests in my arms and in my care.
Sleepily he looks at me.

And I am ashamed.
I see my Lord before me,
But my heart is dry,
A barren desert where love does not bloom.

In the sweet form of Guru, I adore You,
I yearn endlessly, pining as if You are lost,
Yet You are before me,
Wearing green eyes and soft fur.

My eyes partly open, I notice You,
But in the desert of my heart
I fall victim to the wasteland.

I am dry and parched.
My love falls short,
I feel pain where love is lost.

In all the manifest forms
You are dreaming the great Dream,
And I am rejecting You,
Beloved of my heart.

Green eyes are staring at me.
How is it I cannot feel You?
Why is my heart dry
When I hold You in my arms?

May the sweet rain of Your love
Wet this parched desert,
That my heart may bloom
Expanding in love to caress You in all forms.

To move from fear to love, I needed to find acceptance, trust, and faith in Guru/God and the guidance I
was receiving. It required learning the path of love and
surrender, not only in meditation but in the world.
Knowing Guru, God, and Self to be one cosmic existence,
I found myself saying, "I am here. I am yours. Do with
me what you will." I found myself walking a very different path than I had ever dared to tread before: listening
to love rather than fear, listening within rather than to
the world, following the heart rather than the mind. I was
learning to live my life as a tribute to the Divine. To dance
in rhythm with the soft whispers of love and forget all
other influences.

As I shifted my psychology and began to practice
acceptance, my panic attacks stopped, never to return. I
faced the transformation, and, for the first time, I began
to bring my inner mystical life into my outer life. With
this, a profound change began to occur. I began to experience the descent of the Divine towards the earth rather than the rise of *kundalini shakti* towards the Divine. It
would take some years for this transition to manifest fully, but it began with this moment of transformation and
acceptance. I chose to accept Baba's love for me and all
beings and live in Grace, no matter how crazy or outside

of worldly norms and values it may appear. It was a hard choice—but, really, there was no other.

This experience of the descent of divine Grace was and is as if clouds are breaking apart, leaving an opening in the sky where rays of sunlight break through to touch the earth. In the same way, the wave of bliss—I cannot call it other than the grace of God—descends with Baba's words and Baba's presence. My mind and sense of self relax, falling back into the descending presence. White light seems to be everywhere, and that grace or presence flows into me, permeating me for a moment, a minute, an hour.

The mind stills in the wave of this love. There is nothing but the Beloved. It is as if I am dissolved into the descent of divine Presence, which moves into me, through me, permeating the cells of my body, flowing out through words, through waves invisible to the human eye. It creates a space in this world, like sunshine, changing, shifting to light, to love, to a divine Presence in this world. Some see it, feel it. Others do not notice. This I have come to know as Guru Shakti, the presence of the infinite, divine consciousness that my Baba has spoken of.

A Dream and Destiny

The language of dreaming spoke to me one night during this time of transformation. Using the symbols of the psyche, it laid before me a universal mission and the secrets of my awakening.

I dreamt I was a young man in my early twenties with

a very scientific mind, an insatiable curiosity, and a drive for scientific discovery. In the dream, I was a Westerner living in a multistory apartment building. Coming home one day to my room, I found huge, dangerous-looking spiders on the walls. I was frightened, but I remembered I always dealt with them by zapping them with my power ring. Yet when I looked down at my hand, there was no ring. It had been stolen. Frightened by the spiders, I left my apartment and went to talk to a man at the front desk to try to get my ring back, but without success.

The scene changed, and I was with a young woman from one of the other apartments. She was my friend. I believe she came with me as I sought my older brother's help. He was an established scientist, and he was Baba in his manifestation as Taraka Brahma, that tangential guide I mentioned earlier that exists between the manifest and unmanifest universe. In the dream, he lived in a strange place. It was some large scientific, industrial building.

There were wires and catwalks. The young woman and I walked around the building for some time, across the catwalks and up and down ladders, through vast dark empty areas, searching for my brother. Finally, I found him.

When I saw my brother standing in the distance, a vicious wolf-type creature intent on killing me appeared. Knowing I needed to escape, I grabbed the young woman and jumped into a nearby swimming pool to avoid the creature. The pool had a bar of light under it, somewhat like a photocopy machine scanning light, and we had to go to the bottom of the pool to prevent the wolf from getting us.

In the dream, I knew I was on the brink of coming into my power. I also knew that dark forces, represented by the wolves and spiders, wanted to kill and destroy me before I became a threat. They had stolen my power ring to try to stop me. My brother understood what was going on and was helping me through the process.

Now I was beginning to feel my power and had an insatiable scientific curiosity that made me go straight for the danger rather than be thwarted as these wolf-type creatures were jumping in the water to get me. Instead of trying to escape, I went after them.

The next thing I knew, my brother and I were sitting beside the pool, along with the young woman. I told my brother she was my daughter and I needed to protect her. To do this, I had her stay in a cage where these creatures would not be able to get to her and harm her. I loved her and knew she needed protection as I began to realize who I was and what was going on. As I reflect upon this dream, this woman seems to be my current incarnation and the man that I am in the dream appears to represent my deeper self that goes from life to life. My older brother was, of course, Baba.

In the next scene, I returned to my apartment, and my mother was there, not my real mother but a woman who was my mother in the dream. She was with a friend having tea when I entered. It seemed as if it was her apartment, and I lived with her. She said she wanted me to be a good boy and stop what I was doing. She told me

I should be afraid and conform, that I needed to lie down because I was fragile and not well.

She appeared concerned, and, in the past, I had always listened to her, thinking she knew best. But this time, I did not do as she said. I would not succumb to the belief that I was weak and sickly, as I now knew that it was just another false belief to keep me subdued, to stop me from coming into my truth. The forces of darkness knew who I was. They knew I would be extremely dangerous to them if I came into my power. But now, I knew what was happening, and though my power, my Shakti, was just beginning, I would not be swayed. I was going directly after discovering how to conquer these forces of darkness.

My dream brother, whom I had gone to for help, was my elder brother, Baba, Taraka Brahma, and he was teaching me the way to my strength. I was Baba's younger brother, dedicated to the same mission as he was—to fight these forces of darkness in the world.

In the dream, I had been kept in the dark by these forces subduing me. I finally became aware that there had been a battle ensuing my whole life, and I didn't know it. There was a war between the forces of light and those of darkness. I was coming into my own to fight in this battle, to help my elder brother win the war. The most profound aspect of the dream for me was this strong, firm knowledge that I had already come to a place where I could not be defeated, although I was still in the midst of the battle with these forces oppressing me. I perceived the wolf and spiders as representing the cosmic forces of darkness, or ignorance, trying to overcome me.

Then, in the dream, I saw a pyramid. It was much like the pyramid I would see as a child that led to my destiny. As a child, I knew that when I reached the pyramid's apex, I would know my destiny and what I was to do. I saw the same pyramid shape in the dream, but it changed. The shape began to have a narrow opening like a funnel. It reminded me of a birth canal, narrow and then expanding. When I entered the funnel area in the dream, it felt like a transition between what had been and this tremendous force that was opening up inside me.

This dream was significant for me, highlighting the universal and eternal battle in the world—and in each of us—between the forces of darkness or ignorance and those of light and enlightenment. It told me that this mission Baba was guiding me towards, the destiny I had felt my entire life, was to work with him to bring the forces of light into this world. This was the battle dream, the eternal battle played in the minds and hearts of every living being. It was my destiny to battle fear and smallness and, along with my elder brother, to fight to awaken the light in the hearts and minds of living beings.

In the dream, my current manifestation was a woman kept in a cage until my "soul self" was strong enough to keep her safe in this cosmic battle. Dreaming, I realized that I had felt weak, insecure, fearful, and inadequate for most of my life. My "dream self" bought into this idea, thinking I had some affliction until I fought it and came into my own.

I knew the significance of this dream in my process of transformation, and I kept it close to my heart, watching as destiny unfolded.

The First Teachings

Shortly after this dream of destiny, teachings began to flow to me from Baba. My inner guru advised me, "Forget your fear; accept your future. Then your mind will find peace and your heart comfort. There is no other option for you. If others think you are mad, let them. You are for me, not for them. You act out of love, not for name or fame. If these come, also ignore them. Praise and blame are the same; ignore them and be what I request of you. Act for love of the Infinite and no other reason." This solid advice framed my life as the teachings emerged.

The first teachings came to me in early 1991. I was sitting in a small room in my home where I would do my meditation. A window faced outwards with orange trees holding precious fruit in view against the sky. The house was quiet; my children were at daycare and school, and my husband was at work. I reached for my journal, and my inner guide asked me to start writing. He began to talk to me, and as he did, I wrote it down word for word. This process was familiar to me, but what was different was that, for the first time, the words were not just for me.

As he spoke, I wrote, *"In the life of an aspirant, there comes a time when spiritual life is more important than secular interests. At this time, neither friend nor family can fulfill the yearning of the heart…."* I continued transcribing what I was hearing. *"At such a time, no one can comfort, no one can appease the longing. The spiritual seeker becomes heartbroken for the Beloved. When such a feeling comes, there is only one comfort: love from the Supreme."*

The teaching described how grace cannot be attained by discipline or any credentials. *"You cannot earn this grace. It must simply be given."* My guide admonished, *"Never think you are not worthy or that the Divine has no interest in you."* He assured me, *"This is not the case."* He then suggested that surrendering your heart is the way to grace. From this simple teaching, my Baba went on to talk about the transmutation of consciousness.

A month later, the second teaching came. This time it was about the world condition. It began, *"In order for humanity to survive the coming years, many people must become aware of the spiritual nature of the situation. The human heart can and will become expanded. In its sphere, all troubles will find answers. Humans will turn to the ways of love to find solutions to hardships. The earth will become a haven for sentient beings. War will not touch its surface. Life will endure beyond difficult events."*

It went on, and I continued to write the words dropping into my mind, *"In the wake of the hardships, many will seek spiritual comfort. Many will forget material dreams and dream instead of a world ruled by love, a world governed by universal sentiment. Never has such a time existed. All history has built this. Now human society will soon embark on the path of collective upliftment. A new era approaches…. Humanity will survive, and it will build this society. For a thousand years, it will prosper. The age of unity will advance all areas of human endeavor…."*

*"This will bring the opening for interplanetary communica-
tion. Soon the isolated status will end. Human beings will find
they are part of a vast network of developing entities whose very
existence has roots in the conscious mental projection of the cosmic mind. Human beings will gain a true understanding of the
nature of their existence and their duty in the vast network of
sentient life. We are only a small segment of a vast interaction,
a huge manifestation of sentient form, all contained within the
mental sphere of the Supreme."*

This early guidance in 1991 was the first of many predictive statements my guide has made, but they all come
back to this. My Baba saw times of turmoil and difficulty
coming but has consistently affirmed that we will survive
these times, and they will be followed by the new era he
describes above in these very early teachings.

I knew when this came that this was Guru Shakti
manifesting, the grace and guidance of the Infinite One
Self continuing to come to the earth plane, descending
with love and caring for all beings. I felt like a hollow
flute, a vessel through which the teachings flowed, at that
time, into my secret journal. I still had no idea where this
was going.

The months went by, and my divine guide began to
give more teachings. These early teachings, written in my
journal, spoke of the fundamentals of tantra as a spiritual
path and women's hidden potential. They were ideas I
had never entertained. I thought this was channeling I
was doing.

I had heard of channeling and read some channeled

books. But my Baba clarified, saying to me that channeling involved transmission from another entity. He noted this was not channeling, as he was not another entity but an aspect or manifestation of the cosmic mind. He called it "intrapsychic communication," meaning that it is communication between the conscious mind and a deeper level of consciousness arising in the cosmic mind. He says that, like the fingers of a hand, the aspects of cosmic existence appear out of the whole of being. My guide asked me not to think of this as channeling, as it does not involve guidance from a corporal entity but rather a communion with a deeper aspect of cosmic existence.

My experience when Baba talks to me is that it feels as if understanding drops into my mind as a whole knowing and then sorts itself into words as it filters to more concrete aspects of my being, moving from subtle waves to inner words, to speech, ideas that form and manifest. But where it originates is a knowing, a whole beyond words. Often, I feel Baba's blissful presence during the transmission. A wave that stuns the mind and showers light everywhere.

During these early years, I felt shy about my experience and showed the writings to no one, despite Baba's insistence that I make them public. The first person I shared them with was a good friend named Ganesh, who had moved out of the area but returned for a visit. We reconnected at a group meditation, and I told him about my experiences. I showed him a copy of the writings I had received to date, and he got very excited about them. He asked if he could take copies to share with some friends of his. I said, "Okay," and that was that. The writings started to spread through the yoga community grapevine.

Word continued to circulate, and by the beginning of 1992, I was receiving teachings on many subjects. People started to ask questions and would receive answers. The teachings came slowly at this point, the words appearing two or three at a time with a pause and then a few more words. To my endless surprise, these bunches of words formed sentences, and the sentences formed ideas that made sense!

The first person to truly be called by my inner Guide was a yogic nun called *Didi*, or simply Sister, who had heard about the writings. She visited me in 1992 and stayed for a while, asking if she could help. With the two of us present, my inner Baba suggested that I begin to speak what he was saying. As I spoke the words phrase by phrase, Didi wrote them down by hand. After some time, we began to record them and then have them transcribed. These transcribed writings became called the IW, Inspired Writings. Different people began to take copies of the teachings and quietly spread them around to their friends.

Inner Experience

Slowly my inner experience of spiritual presence existed not only in my meditation but equally, if not more so, in becoming the vehicle of these divinely inspired teachings. When my inner Baba would descend towards the earth plane, opening the clouds of material existence, the light of divine Presence would shine forth for me, and I would feel the unity of all beings.

Then a new revelation began to unfold, and my spiritual experience changed. It had previously focused on my personal relationship with the Divine. Now it began to include mystical experiences of people around the globe. While Baba once told me that I would come to love his children deeply, I was aware that I was most attached to God/Guru/Guide, my family, and close friends. Yet, for the first time, I began to feel people in the unitary whole of being, present, like waves within my mind.

Lying down in my bed or on the floor of my meditation room, looking out the window at the orange tree and blue sky, Baba's divine Presence would surround me. As my mind expanded, a sense of the presence of living beings would arise, like a web of life. People would appear in my consciousness like waves rising out of the ocean. This experience would come during the day, in the evening, anytime. I would fall into it, the presence of different people flowing into my awareness. A knowingness would arise, unfolding what was going on with them, what they were feeling, thinking. The feeling of the person would exist in awareness and then subside, part of an interwoven, interconnected whole of being. I felt that all the people were within me. Everything was within me.

Retreat

As word got out and people intrigued with the writings began to visit, the transmission process grew smoother, and the teachings became more frequent. A small group gathered around the talks and transcribed writings, enjoying feeling in Baba's presence when the flow came. One friend, Van, offered to print a booklet of the writings to give out at an upcoming retreat. This was an exciting project, and we were all into it.

However, before the retreat rolled around, a few people began to have ominous and, as it turned out, prophetic dreams. One woman, Sumitra, dreamed that we were the Christians going into the lion's den—a rather explicit dream, not hard to interpret. Another man, Krsna, had a dream before the retreat that Baba was flying in a helicopter. There were two other helicopters behind his with the orange-robed monks in them. The helicopters were flying overhead when Krsna, on the ground with several of us, started looking up.

Suddenly Baba's helicopter spun out of control and fell to the earth, blowing up in flames near where we were standing. In the dream, Krsna felt suspicious that the monks in the other copters had something to do with it. Everyone was frightened, thinking that Baba was dead, but then Baba came walking, unscathed, out of the flames. He was smiling as he walked to us, hands in prayer position, giving the namaskar greeting to everyone! Simultaneously, the other two helicopters with the monks in them kept flying into the distance without Baba. These dreams seemed to be both symbolic and predictive of Baba's actions and the reactions of the monks in charge.

The international yoga and meditation retreat we were all going to was scheduled for summer. It turned out that the official leaders from India would be at this retreat due to its international orientation. I had not been to a big retreat since all of this happened and was looking forward to the meditations and devotional spirit I knew would be there. The Inspired Writings books came with my friend Van in the back of his car. The retreat was the first public announcement of the IW teachings' existence.

Reactions

As if my trepidation at first receiving the teachings was not enough, once I gained a small bit of confidence from the positive feedback and supportive people that surrounded me, to whom these teachings had become deeply meaningful, the existing power structure of the larger international community went after me.

At the retreat, the reaction by the monks in charge was extreme. We had a meeting during the retreat with ten or so people supporting the writings and important monks from India and America who, along with a few lay people, opposed the writings. A horrible scene ensued in which one monk in charge compared me to Salman Rushdie, the famous author who wrote *The Satanic Verses* and inflamed Ayatollah Khomeini, who issued a *fatwa*, or edict, against him, calling for his assassination.

With a stern look and angry, shaking voice, this orange-robed swami fervently threatened me, "Look what happened to Salman Rushdie for the writings he brought forward!" The monk then admonished me that no one must ever see the book of IW Writings. None of these teachings can be known by anyone.

This monk in charge not only compared me to Salman Rushdie, but he also compared himself to the Ayatollah. Ironically, apparently unbeknownst to this swami, Anandamurti Baba had spoken out against the Ayatollah and said that the Ayatollah made three mistakes, and Salman Rushdie made one. The Ayatollah made the mistake of not reading the writings. (The monks had not read the IW either.) He also made the mistake of banning them and then threatening the author. But Salman Rushdie made one mistake only: he apologized. This, Anandamurti Baba said, weakened Rushdie's message. Well, that was an interesting turn and seemed like guidance on how to respond as things went forward, which they did.

Then these orange-robed swamis, with their orange turbans and long beards, proceeded to tell us outright that these teachings could not exist. They feared they would split the organization and diminish their authority. They proclaimed that no one should see these writings and banned us from handing them out.

It was their event, and we needed to follow their instructions. Yet a number of people approached me, wanting to hear the teachings, so we held sessions to share them. Many people showed sincere interest. They desperately wanted to see the writings, so Van let it be quietly known that he had left the trunk of his car open. Somehow, one by one, all 250 copies of the book he had brought with him disappeared from the trunk.

After the retreat, in an all-out effort to suppress any interest in these teachings, the powers that be spread disinformation and took loyalty oaths from people against the IW teachings. Anyone who spoke out in favor of the teachings was reprimanded or began to be excluded. On Mother's Day of 1994, I received a call telling me I had been officially expelled and could no longer go to community functions. I was banned, and anyone who had anything to do with me was getting serious repercussions. One by one, others who supported the IW were either excommunicated or told not to come anymore. People were forced to choose between staying with the existing community or following the IW. It was not fair to anyone—or necessary.

This process of suppression and persecution created a rift between people. Those people who had experienced Guru's spiritual presence in these writings and discourses could not deny their feelings. They were put in an awkward position. There was a rejection of people's pleas to listen. Thus, a rift developed that I was unable to do anything about.

On a deeper, internal level, I had deep experiences of the unity of all beings. And when I felt people, one against another in this kind of rejection of other people's personal experiences, it hurt. It was very painful, as if something sweet and precious was being torn apart by bigotry and narrow-mindedness. That it was happening so unnecessarily for political reasons deeply saddened me.

This was a devotional flow of teachings stemming from love for the Divine and the grace of Guru. It had no political motive. But I was a Western married woman, and the organization's leadership consisted of Indian monks who had been near the physical guru and ran the community. To them, unfortunately, it was not just political but also a threat. This led to division, and Baba guided me, saying he must provide shelter for those turned away from their spiritual home.

On one level, it was a tragedy for everyone. On another, it seemed destined to be. A movement, a flow of cosmic energies on a path that could not be other than what it was. So, I have found it is with many events in life, much like the classic Taoist parable of the farmer whose horse ran away while he labored in his fields.

In the parable, the farmer's neighbors, on hearing the news that he lost his horse, said, "How sad, how awful. How tragic for your family." The farmer replied, "Maybe yes, maybe no." Then, when the farmer woke the next morning, his horse had returned with several wild horses it brought back to the farmer. The neighbors, in awe, said, "How wonderful. You are so fortunate!" The farmer again replied, "Maybe yes, maybe no."

After some weeks, the farmer's son broke his leg falling off one of the new horses he was taming. The neighbors all sympathized and bemoaned the farmer's ill luck saying, "How awful!" The farmer again responded, "Maybe yes, maybe no." A few days later, the army came through, conscripting all the eligible young men, but they could not take this farmer's son due to his broken leg. Again, the neighbors came around saying, "Isn't that great!" and the farmer said, "Maybe."

It is hard to know what destiny will unfold, what is truly a tragedy, and what is a blessing. So, I began to accept and leave control of events up to the Divine. After some time, I feared for my life, as I knew what some could do in their passion. Indeed, at one point I was warned by the U. S. State Department of a threat to my life due to my standing up and putting forth these teachings.

However, early on in this process, my husband had a dream that I felt was Baba's message. In the dream, Liam saw a great house burning. Yet I sat quietly, peacefully, in one room of the house, by the light of a single candle, writing. My room in the house was completely untouched by the flames that burned all around me. I remained surrounded by a feeling of protection and grace, the fire controlled by the single candle flame I read by. When I heard about Liam's dream, I knew no harm would come to me—and it did not.

A New Community Forms

This difficult situation led to guidance from Baba in the IW to form a nonprofit community, one that would give spiritual shelter to people and be a base for continued teachings. From my Baba's guidance flowed years of involvement with this new community of friends, many retreats, years of ongoing teachings from the Baba flow, and the training of Acharyas, or meditation teachers, in Baba's system of meditation practices. This became my life.

While I continued to raise my children, work as a psychologist, and lead a family life, much of my time now became devoted to the community that was forming around the spiritual teachings I was receiving. Slowly, as my Baba had said would happen, my love for Guru began to spread to love and attachment to his children.

Giving Baba's Teachings, Community, Acharya Trainings, Yoga Teacher Trainings, Yoga Therapy Trainings & Retreats Became my Life as the Years Unfolded

How the Divine Manifests

As time passed, the guidance I received from the Divine was only getting clearer and more frequent. After a few years, with the increased teachings and spiritual presence, my internal guide began to teach me a new process I had not previously known. One day my guide told me, "I want to teach you a new process by which you can receive my guidance and share it with others." He said he wanted me to listen with my ears to my voice speaking his words, rather than hearing them in my mind and then communicating them. This way, the flow of teachings could be spoken directly with my voice rather than into my mind and then repeated verbally.

Instructions came to "simply relax and allow me to speak with your voice rather than your mental voice. Listen with your ears rather than listening internally." When I first began to try this process, it was very awkward. I was worried that I would not be able to tell if it was my ego speaking or Baba. How was I to know if the teachings were really from Baba? Was I receiving them correctly?

These doubts began to hinder my ability to learn the process that my Baba was trying to teach me. As I struggled with this, I thought I would have to return to the old way of hearing the teachings in my mind. However, as time went on, over the next year and a half, with my guide's continued encouragement, I slowly learned to use this new process.

When the teachings come from my Baba, the experience is different from my normal thought process. During my daily interactions, or even while giving a class, I have a sense of thinking and reasoning when I speak. This is not present when Baba talks, just a flow welling up from deep within, without filters, thoughts, or reason. There is no planning what I will say. I do not even know what the first sentence will be as I begin to speak. I think of my Baba, and it just flows. It is in the moment. Needless to say, I have had to learn to trust this divine guide explicitly, unconditionally. The blissful presence that often accompanies the flow makes the words almost irrelevant at times and is certainly not there when I speak from the conscious, rational mind.

When I finally learned to speak directly without acting as an interpreter, several interesting things happened. First, the pauses between words became less, the rhythm becoming a natural flow of language. Second, for many years my Baba began to speak with the inflections and tones that Anandamurti Baba had used in his physical life. I found that interesting. The teachings began to feel purer. To me, it felt more like Guru was speaking directly, making the process more vibrant. It seemed to be clearer and richer for other people as well.

As times have changed, the accent with external voice has all but fallen away. But in the 1990s, when Baba's flow spoke to other people, there was a phraseology, a style of talking, different from mine. There was also the distinct feeling of "other." While I have come to wonder whether Baba's accent was a matter of devotional sentiment, it was nevertheless charming, and perhaps it even served a purpose. The soft, lilting tone and style of speaking expressed a sweetness, and a subtlety of vibration, that brought forward the experience of his presence. In recent years the flow has changed: the lilting sweetness is there, but the accent is rarely present. My guide has recently taught me to keep my eyes open and look at people when the flow comes. This has been challenging, as I lose the flow if distracted. But I am learning.

As time passes, I have felt more blending of Baba's presence in this body-mind structure I call my own. Like an old friend, this cosmic presence is so familiar that my mind slides into it/him, and I cannot find the difference between us. In these moments, the experience of my small self dissolves, and only the rich flow of divine wisdom and love I know to be Baba is there. In this body, in that moment, is *Ma*, one with Baba's divine aspect. Then it passes, the teaching moment is over, and I re-form into the consciousness of self and others.

I am a very ordinary person in this world. Yet in my normal waking state, I remember. I remember there is only one deep unitary whole in which we all exist. I have realized that this world I once considered mundane is far from ordinary. It is the vibrant expression of divine existence, manifesting as the light and shadows of creation. A single blade of grass, a moment, or even a footstep are embodiments of eternal Being. And, to think that I once thought it mundane, apart from God.

Chapter XII
A Taste of Grace

Offering myself to You
Beloved Husband of my heart
Humbly I come to Your feet.

Dear beyond description
Your eyes hold me.
Seeing you, my heart opens.

From the depths of my being
My soul goes forth,
Immersed in longing from the heart
I reach out to be met by You.

Taking my hand
You enfold me in Your being
I lose all sense of boundary
Looking into Your eyes, all dissolves.

There is nothing but You.
In the vastness of infinite space
In the innermost recesses of the human heart
In every molecule of existence
You alone abide.

All is Your reflection,
I am, but Your expression.
You are the Dreamer.
All else is the dream.

I find there is only expansiveness, an endless ocean of compassion and grace. I cannot find where this experience has any limitations. The only limitations are my own, my fears, and my apprehension to let go completely, fully, and become that which I love. The limitations lie in the ego, in the messages I tell myself—or we all tell ourselves—messages that hold a sense of ownership of all of our mental constructs.

I have believed that I am defined by my thoughts, by beliefs that I have acquired about myself. I have had a feeling of possessiveness, that the ideas and the limitations I have acquired belong to me. The challenge to me—and to us all, in spiritual life—is, can we really let go of these limitations we have identified with? Can we clear our minds of our conditioned ideas so that our eyes can see the vision of the one true and gracious God/Self?

It is my experience that this capacity to clear the mind of self-deluded thoughts and beliefs is usually beyond our limited human efforts. We tend to circle round and round in the reality we have constructed from our lifetimes of experience. The exit from our self-constructed world is difficult to find. My experience is that it tends to come by the grace of the Infinite One. That One makes Itself known to us, utilizing whatever means may be at hand to awaken the spirit from slumber and the mind from dreams and delusions. That one true Self I have come to know as the Beloved, as my Baba. Others have come to use such words as God, Satguru, Great Spirit, Self, Awareness, Cosmic Consciousness, and so on. In reality, all are simply different names for the same divine, omniscient, aware Beingness.

As a gracious gift of this awakened presence that I refer to as my beloved Baba, many teachings have manifested. They have come through this form that I had thought of as my own. I have had the privilege of seeing the Beloved move, not only in the depths of meditation but also in the world with people, their lives, and their hearts. I have felt most astounded and very humbled to be given the privilege to experience these divine movements and watch that one work to bring all beings from darkness to light, from delusion to wisdom.

Let me share with you a few of the experiences that have touched me with a sense of grace and awe as the flow of these teachings and presence has unfolded in my life.

Dancing with the Divine

In the early years, when the flow of teachings and guidance was first manifesting, a yogic nun named Ananda Deviika Ma came to stay with me. I affectionately called her Didi or Sister. When I first met her, she was going through deep internal struggles about her relationship to her spiritual community. As a nun or sannyasin, dedicated to her guru and the order of nuns he had established, she was experiencing conflicts and doubts which were causing her turmoil and crisis. She had a deep dedication to her guru but had conflicting feelings about the dictates of the nuns' order and organization to which she belonged. These contradictory feelings had caused her a great deal of pain for several years, and she could not seem to put the pain behind her.

Then one day, while she was visiting me, we decided to take a trip to the California coast. When we arrived, we soon found a stand of wind-swept trees growing on a high cliff overlooking the ocean, about sixty feet above the beach. Below us was a rocky California coastline, ocean waves crashing on the shore. The ocean air was filled with the smell of the sea and the sound of gulls calling in the distance.

We sat down on a log under the trees, and Didi asked to speak with Baba through me. I closed my eyes and sank deep into the inner space where Baba dwells. My mind becoming lost in him, I began to talk, feeling his love and care for my friend. Baba's words flowed through me in the wave of this love, addressing her struggles.

Unbeknownst to me, as this guidance began, Didi saw Baba materialize before her, dressed as he would have been in his physical life in a white kurta, Indian shirt, and *dhoti*, a traditional pant. He stood before her, radiating love, compassion, and spiritual light. Then, as he placed his hand upon her head, a blissful feeling of divine Grace began to permeate her, and he said, "From now on, I will guide you."

She told me afterward that when this happened, she felt all the confusion and concerns about her situation disappear, and her karmic patterns dissolve. She said that, to her great relief, she felt that her burdens had been lifted, and her life changed—that she was now in Guru's hands and not those of any organization.

As I slowly came out of the deep immersion in Guru's flow, the bliss of his presence still permeating me, Ananda Deviika Ma shared with me what had happened during the guidance. I was stunned and amazed. I knew it was Grace, and I felt honored and humbled to see this divine guide at work.

Then some months later, I was amazed when Ananda Deviika Ma told me that her profound inner change had continued as time passed. When I checked in with her and asked her how she was, she said, "All the trouble I had been experiencing is gone. Baba took it from me during that session, and it has never returned."

I have also noticed that when I have sought personal advice from Baba's spiritual form over the years, he gives it with understanding and insight far beyond anyone I have met. Now I saw that this also seemed to be the case for Didi. I have found this inner guru to be a master psychologist who looks into one's core and weaves the deepest insights into his guidance.

Grace at a Retreat

A man I did not know at the time, Hari, a commercial pilot and longtime Baba devotee, had started hearing about something happening in California and decided to come with his friend Bob to a retreat. What follows is a tale of his experience, which he relayed some years later.

Hari had heard that someone in California could channel Baba's presence. It didn't sound too illogical to him because his wife Isla and he had read *A Course in Miracles,* a book believed to be a dictation by Jesus to, interestingly enough, a female Jewish psychologist. Hari found it powerful when he read it. So, he thought, "Why couldn't this also be possible?"

Being curious, Hari got his friend Bob a buddy pass, and they headed west. They didn't know if the rumor was true, but they assured each other that, even if there were nothing to it, they would have a weekend vacation together, and it would be a blast. When Hari and Bob got to the retreat, Hari thought it was at an amazing spot, somewhere north of Santa Cruz, with ocean views and natural beauty.

Hari told us, "I remember that it was a unique group. Immediately I felt at home with everyone. Yet after the first evening, Bob and I thought the retreat was nothing special and that we might leave the next day. But there hadn't been a Baba talk yet, so we thought we should at least stick around for the session the next morning before leaving."

Hari sat back, smiled, and then commented, "I can never forget the moment that this talk began. The flow that I felt was so, so, so strong. First, we did kirtan, chanting divine names, and then we did our meditation. By the time the talk started, let's just say I had never felt something quite so strong. I remember seeing Bob going into samadhi, a trance, and others feeling the same energy. I may have been in samadhi myself without knowing it. It was extremely deep. I could see energy everywhere I looked. It was like a veil had been lifted. I remember Andy—we didn't know each other, but suddenly, we were hugging each other. And we were feeling this energy that was in the air."

"I can never forget; I think Chuck was the cook that day. And for quite some time, I had a suspicion that he had put LSD or peyote or something in our food because suddenly, this magical window was opening. My heart was opened, and I could feel love everywhere. I knew for sure that Baba was my guru."

Hari reflected, "That was the beginning of this new phase of learning, many trips to the West Coast, sitting by the fire, learning from this Baba flow. At some point, I was inspired to take Acharya training to become a meditation teacher in this tradition. I don't know how I passed my Acharya exam, but I truly got it when Baba said, 'It's what's in your heart,' and he gave me the blessing of passing that along to others."

***

During the same retreat, amidst the beauty of the Northern California coastline, I, too, experienced the amazing presence and shower of love we were all caught in. I came to the retreat with my husband—a little hassled by all the preparations to get things going and anxious about being on the spot to give Baba's flow of guidance. The first evening I asked not to be scheduled to talk. I wanted space to meditate in order to get into the flow. In the morning, I was on.

As always, I have no idea what will happen or what I will say. I feel nervous. It takes a great deal of trust to get up before a group of people who have expectations when I have no plan, no preparation, nothing but trust in my divine guide. After meditating, I walk in and sit down in the designated chair reserved for me. I close my eyes and focus on my guide. Baba is saying to me, "Let me have form." I open up to this divine energy and feel myself melting into Baba—and I begin to talk, simply saying whatever comes into my mind.

I speak four or five words, still having no idea what I will say, or where it is going. Then I feel I am moving into a flow. Words form sentences, form thoughts. I begin to feel a blissful wave and the words flow with the wave. It deepens. A profound love absorbs my mind. As the words flow, they become the reality I am living in. There is only one eternal Being, appearing to be many, in the dance of creation. It is as if this has always been the truth I live in. There is no other.

The words flow and continue in rhythm with the truth, the love, the eternal essence. I see all those around me as divine beings. Part of the One True Self. The words of love flow, forming like drops of nectar in my mind, in my heart. They spill out. Love overflows.

Baba stops; I stop. The talk is over. A wave of white light and ecstatic bliss fills me and stuns my mind. Love overflows. I arise to my senses and look about me. Everyone is in the wave, the bliss palpable. Love abounds. Time has passed. There is a call to lunch. I get up and go to the dining hall. Many stay behind, still lost in the bliss.

I sit to eat, raising my fork to my mouth, but I forget as my mind veers off into ecstatic light. Then returning, I notice the fork still in midair. Aware of the body, I begin to eat. I still cannot talk. Slowly, as the body takes over, the mind returns—but my heart still sings in love. Those around me are laughing, hugging, filled with joy. It is one of those moments.

In the Bliss Giving Baba's Talk

Today, as I write this many years later, an online talk with a few people has just finished, and I feel much the same. The One Eternal Self is all that is. It is as if I have always known this, though, in reality, the experience of it often fades shortly after the talk as my conscious awareness returns to the experience of sensory duality. Yet the knowledge remains in my mind, even when it is not my direct experience of the moment. Such has been the blessing of this exposure.

Not all talks are about the eternal nature of the Self, and my own awareness does not always enter a state of bliss. Some talks are about more practical subjects. Yet, even then, my loving guide always manages to slip in some divine reference—and listeners, to one degree or another, follow the wave to the shores of the Infinite.

Meditation Teacher Training

When the new community that my inner guide, Baba, suggested we form was established, he then began to say there would be a need for people to teach meditation practices and that he wanted us to establish Acharya, or meditation teacher, training. When Baba said that he would personally train the first groups of teachers, word got out, and a number of people came forward. They were all devotees of Baba Anandamurti who had followed the physical guru and studied his work for many years.

The students entered a two-year training process to become established in their own meditation practice as well as the spiritual and social philosophies Shrii Shrii

Anandamurti Baba had given. The training was to be divided into a series of two-week sessions with home-study programs in between.

I was concerned about teaching these sessions, worried that I would not be able to come through for people. I didn't know how Baba's flow could possibly give all of these teachings, and I didn't think that this would really happen. So, once again, my skeptical side got distressed about the reality of doing this training. But, regardless, I followed what Baba said and set up the training.

I arrived at the first training session, and, again, doubts boiled up in my mind. I thought, "Oh my God, is this really going to happen? I can't believe I am doing this. I cannot imagine this actually going forward." But somehow, by divine grace, it did.

Still involved in my worldly life, I was trying to balance my feelings about being a householder, living in the world, being a professional working woman, and having mystical experiences, including this incredible, vibrant, mystical flow of Guru/God coming through. I have found this flow unlike anything else I have ever known in my life, because I do not experience doing it! It is as if it is doing itself. It is manifesting for other people and interfacing and interacting with them. Yet there is no feeling of "doer-ship" on my part, no sense that I have anything to do with the flow of these teachings.

My experience is that this is not a human force. This is not something of human life; it is something quite different. All that a human being can be is kind of a lightning rod or conduit through which this force can be attracted or channeled into the world, but the conduit or lightning rod does little except to simply be present and available.

To perceive the presence of this force defied my constructs of reality. Although I've been a mystical person all my life, I think fundamentally, deep inside, I've been an atheist. I believed there was a unitive consciousness, but what I didn't believe in was a power or force in the universe that could care, love, heal, and guide. I think I truly had trouble believing in this. Concepts like God or a divine Power were, in a way, theoretical to me.

But the skeptic within me became highly challenged by all of my experiences of Baba, more so than by anything else in my life, because I have directly seen this divine Force interceding and interacting in the world. With this ever-unfolding experience of a divine Presence, a power in the universe, a true power, things began to change. When the meditation or Acharya training happened, all my skeptical doubts and fears had to be put aside in the face of what was manifesting.

During Training

The site we found for the training was a house in Santa Cruz that belonged to a friend of mine, a beautiful home directly on the Pacific. In fact, right across the street, there were some small cliffs, about twenty feet high, beyond which lay the ocean. The front room where the training was conducted was surrounded on three sides by glass, with a balcony across the front, creating a most spectacular atmosphere. You could see the beautiful blue water and hear the continual, gentle sound of the waves during the entire training. In fact, the ocean was so much a part of the atmosphere in this room that it almost felt as if we were on a boat.

There were twelve students for this first training, and as it began, as usual, I felt nervous. As I have said, I could not imagine how my Baba was going to do this. Prior to this training, I'd had only the experience of having Baba come for an hour, or hour and a half at the most, and give a discourse, but my experience was about to change radically.

As we sat down at the training, my Baba began to give discourses through me on the meaning of being a family Acharya and point out, with insight, the details of what it means to put oneself in the position of being a spiritual teacher. He explained to these potential teachers what that commitment was about and what responsibilities to other people involved. In his intuitive talks, my Baba presented a most noble way of life, a most inspiring ideal that everyone who was at the training was very taken with.

As the training went on, my guide began to go into the depths of the teachings and talk about the subtleties of the kundalini experience and about subtle body theories: the kundalini process, the chakras, the *pranas,* and the *nadiis* in the body, other aspects of subtle body theory. He expounded upon mantras, the *koshas,* teaching meditation, and other relevant subjects. I had little prior knowledge of some of the subjects. But I would learn, as others did, by listening to the discourses coming through this body I had called my own.

We did long hours of immersive meditation, averaging about six hours a day. The Baba flow often happened after the meditations and would go on for several hours at a stretch. As the training went on, the flow of divine energy and teachings from Baba was manifesting through my physical form for at least five or six hours a day. After a few days of this, I began to feel ill from so much Shakti, to experience a burning heat throughout my body, exhaustion, and nausea. I became worried that I was being burned up by kundalini shakti and that the amount of energy that was coming into my body from the Baba flow was beyond its physical endurance.

In addition, the next morning, when I was doing my *pranayama*, breath practices, a fear arose as my focus entered the *Anahata chakra*, heart center. I began to worry that my intense concentration might affect my heart. I began to fear that somehow the guidance I was receiving wasn't clear, that I was doing something wrong. I began to be inundated with doubts.

And so, in the privacy of my room, I asked my internal guide how to deal with all of this. In response, Baba said that my fear was due to my doubt but that I should not worry—the discomfort I was having would pass, and there would be no permanent difficulty. So, I continued to teach, and the bodily discomforts seemed to fade away as I adjusted to the long hours spent in the *bhava*, the immersive state that was necessary for the teachings to flow.

Then, in the sessions that followed, Baba's flow was addressing spiritual practices in realms of which I had no personal knowledge, and people were recording what was being said. Then they were taking videos. It all began to be too much for me. I wanted to run away from the whole situation.

Afraid of giving inaccurate information, I went to Baba again internally and said, "Baba, please help me. I am afraid of walking in your shoes, wearing your mantle. I am afraid I can't do it. I can't meet up to their needs. I can't hold this. Oh, Baba, it scares me. I am ready to give my life in service. I am ready to dissolve my individuality so that they can have Guru again, but I am frightened that I cannot hold this. I am frightened that I'll let them down. I'm frightened that I am not always a hundred percent clear. Oh, Baba, this is a lot to come at me. They want you so badly; they love you so much. How can I hold this for you?"

Baba responded to me, "I will tell you. You hold it not at all. I am the only one capable to shoulder this. You need only to defer to me and to my judgment. Your problem is doubt; due to a weakness in trust, you experience fear and doubt. These are your enemies. When they arise, know you are deficient in faith or trust. Emphasize trust and love—and doubt and fear will fade. I will review the chakras for you, so you may feel more secure. Your fear comes because you begin to doubt what you have been given, and then you begin to fear a public error. From that arises fear for your physical heart, a fear already strong within you. In pranayama, thoughts are intensified, and so this was intensified. You must resolve it by trusting me."

With this guidance, I gathered my courage and went out again to face everybody and to sit and again allow Baba to give yet another discourse on spiritual teachings. I found that the heat, exhaustion, fear, and ill feelings began to pass. As they melted away, an incredible bliss came over me. It was the joy of divine presence. I had never before known this divine presence so strongly and so beautifully as I knew it then. I bathed in a sense of complete safety, complete security, wholeness, bliss, waves of well-being, and ecstasy. I felt I was made of light, that this body was transmuted into light itself, that there was light everywhere.

When Baba spoke, I felt waves of divine energy emanating from him, filling the room with light, bliss, and love. After Baba would speak, trainees would do sadhana, and even when lunch came, many often continued their meditation. Though they were called for food, they were reluctant to leave the bliss they were experiencing. Slowly, one by one, finally, they would get up and drift in for their meal.

From then on, the rest of the training became one ecstatic flow for me. Baba's divine Presence manifested not only in my meditation but whenever my Beloved spoke. When he spoke, I would feel light everywhere. Bliss and ecstasy would fill me. The words would be expressions of divine Presence, ecstatic existence. The teaching and knowledge would be as if it unfolded from the body of ecstatic being, flowed into me, and out again through the voice of this body.

All of us at the training were caught in this wave of ecstasy and unconditional love. Long meditations each morning, walks on the beach in the afternoon, talking, sharing, deeply bonding friendships brought closeness among everyone. Baba's talks in the morning, in the afternoon, in the evening, our weeks together formed into a time of deep spiritual beauty that was, for every person present, most profound.

There was no conflict, no tension. It was as if Baba's wave washed away all the individual ego problems that would otherwise have arisen among people living in such close quarters. We moved together in a kind of harmony. The best and the noblest aspects of each person were brought to the surface by this divine Presence. Though quarters were tight, everyone got along, and events flowed smoothly. People easily maintained silence each morning, and the wave of bliss and unity that was felt collectively was unlike anything I had ever heard of or experienced.

I became a person held in the arms of the Beloved. Carried on a wave of ecstatic existence, all that I had ever been was as if suspended, and I was there, in that moment, in that love. Then as the training continued, Baba began to stay in this body, in this mind, for longer and longer periods of time. After a while, most of the day was spent immersed in the bhava, the flow of his presence.

Toward the end of the training, Baba told me he would give personal sessions with each trainee. This again caused me some trepidation, but this time I let go and flowed with it. When I sat in these private sessions with each individual, I felt this body, this mind, filled with sattvic sentience, pure and sweet. I felt radiant white light everywhere. As my Beloved spoke with people through this form, words just came. I had no notion of their meaning, or lack of meaning, to anyone. I only knew it was my Beloved speaking. This body simply spoke the words that were there to be said. For me, it has taken a huge leap of faith to allow this body to speak these comments when I have no idea if they have any meaning or relevance.

During these personal sessions, I would feel Baba's presence, his tone, his wave, his charm, his unconditional love, and his sweetness. Loving kindness and compassion would overflow. Then my Baba would begin speaking to each person, and what he said would be very personal. I would not know the context of his words to anyone until afterward, and only if they chose to share their experiences. It was by their narrations that I became aware of the little miracles happening for each person he had spoken with. Through this body, in these private sessions, the guru of my heart helped each trainee with their problems.

Chapter XII: A Taste of Grace

Training

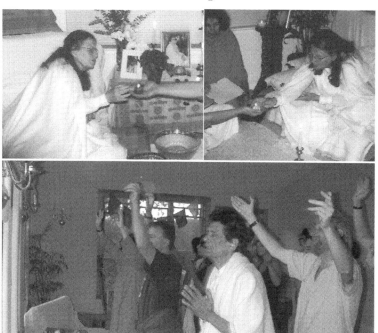

Training, Kirtan & Retreats

249

Training, Kirtan & Retreats

The Walk

Toward the end of the training, the students asked if Baba would do something called a field walk, which was something that Shrii Shrii Anandamurti Baba had done in his physical form. In his years as a physical guru, Anandamurti Baba would go on a walk with people and talk while he walked. Much to my surprise and distress, my Baba agreed to do this. So, it was arranged that near the end of the training, we would all take a late-night walk together after the evening program. We decided that we would walk by the ocean.

I had a great deal of trepidation about this; I really didn't know how this would go. I had only been in the presence of the Baba flow sitting with my eyes closed, and I knew very well I could not go for a long walk at night with my eyes closed. I had no idea how to give Baba's talk with eyes open and walking, no less!

The night finally came; it was late, perhaps ten or eleven. We put on our coats and shoes, preparing for the cold January night. Slipping outside, breath frosting, we could see moonlight on the path; but the ocean we headed towards was deep and dark, a midnight blue. As we crossed the street towards the sea, my guide said to me, "Now I will enter the physical form and walk this night."

I felt Baba come near to me, his presence filling my mind. Then I noticed that this body was walking quickly, and that other people were falling behind. My eyes were open to see the moonlit path I walked. People were asking questions, and Baba was responding. Emotionally this was quite difficult for me. Walking and talking with eyes open, I felt quite my usual self, so I began to worry, "If I feel so normal, how can this be Baba who is speaking? I don't feel as if I am in an altered state of consciousness or that anything unusual is happening."

I began to worry, "Is this pure? Is this really Baba? Is it clear? Am I talking? Is this Baba talking?" So, uncertain, I listened carefully to Baba's mental words and then repeated what he said. I was afraid to let him speak, worrying that it wasn't clear because I was walking and talking.

Then, after what had previously been a very difficult walk to a beach area that I thought was far away, our destination suddenly was in front of us. I had no idea how we had gotten there so quickly. I didn't feel tired at all, even though previously I had had trouble walking to this area. We spent some time at the beach and then turned around to walk back to the house. I remained in Baba's flow. Then during the walk back, we stopped at a bench, and in the bhava, the flow of Baba's presence, I sat down and continued talking for a time before moving on.

When we got back to the house, I was energized, not tired. It seemed that this outing had hardly taken any time, even though Baba had been speaking continuously and I had been undergoing a certain amount of mental tension during the trip, as the skeptic in me had risen to the surface. When the Baba flow passed, and I was present again as the one expressing through this body, I noticed people were laughing. I asked what they were laughing about. They told me I had been walking so fast that they had to run to keep pace with me!

I had no idea that was occurring. They said they found it so amusing because Anandamurti Baba, in his physical form, had also walked very quickly—something, again, I was only partially aware of. But it delighted them, so I was happy. The trainees also noted that they were pleased with what Baba had said to them while walking. I was a bit mystified by the whole experience, but I realized my uncertainty, doubt, and skepticism were my issues and that I did not need to let my difficulties interfere with their experience.

When this first training session ended, the degree to which I had delved into the cauldron of divine nectar to experience the presence of the divine Beloved had expanded far beyond anything I had previously thought could occur. Yet, as Baba had foretold from the very beginning, this was not the end nor the boundary of the depth of this experience. Many more trainings, retreats, and other spiritual events would follow.

The Mystic Night Walk with Baba's Presence

The Trainers Receive Gifts from Trainees as Training Ends
Ananda Maetreyii Ma & Ananda Deviika Ma

When this first training finished and everyone flew
away to their respective homes, I was left again to return

from this ecstatic state of immersion into family life and worldly work at the developmental center. There was a process of reintegrating into worldly life that would repeatedly happen over the years as I left trainings, retreats, and other events where the divine immersion in Baba occurred. I learned to live with the change from the ecstatic presence of the Beloved to practical day-to-day life, though the contrast was, at times, difficult. When I was away from the flow of Baba's guidance for too long, my heart would ache for him, for the opportunity to feel his manifest presence.

A Phone Call

One day, some years later, Jenny, one of the students we had trained, called me in a dilemma. Living in Baltimore, she was driving to another city to help a sick relative. On the way, she stopped at a phone booth along the road and called me to talk to Baba. She was having marital problems and needed help. When she spoke to my Baba through me, the guidance came that she should turn around and return home immediately. She objected that the relative's family was expecting her and that she was already several hours into her trip. Much to my discomfort, my Baba said she could do as she pleased, but if she wanted to save her marriage, she needed to return home.

Jenny struggled with this advice but decided to go home. I had no idea why Baba had given her this guidance, and I felt worried that this would inconvenience

Jenny for no good reason. However, the next day I found out that a difficult situation that had been going on with her husband came to the surface that very night when Jenny got home. Her being there for him when it all came out was critical to their relationship, allowing them to stay together in a long and happy marriage. I felt enormous gratitude for being able to watch this spiritual flow of guidance dance in the world, loving and caring, not only for me but for others as well.

Baba's Grace

Many years have passed since these experiences, and I have continued to observe this divine Beloved assisting other people, often resolving issues—not just temporarily, but many times permanently. I continue to be amazed when I see this divine flow at work.

Though I am often unaware of the relevance of what is being said during the talks or private sessions, I have repeatedly discovered that the words have meaning to the people or persons to whom my guide is speaking. I am awed by the capacity of this subtle intuitive existence, manifesting in this body that I have known to be my own. I do not know how these things happen, but, as I have said, I feel honored and humbled to witness it.

In the process of receiving this intuitional flow, it is as if a hole opens in the clouds. All misperceptions of the nature of reality fall away. Everything that my guide says becomes my experience. I believe perhaps this happens for some others as well. I find empowerment in the words. There is a radiance of light, and I feel I am in Guru's presence. The experience is difficult to describe, but it really wouldn't matter if the talks were coming through this physical form, which I also happen to inhabit, or through another physical form. It seems to me it would be the same experience. I listen with my ears, as anyone else would listen, and I receive darshan, presence.

When my Baba has embodied—in this form I have known as my own—for an extended period, as I have noted, a wave of pure sentience, so refined that it seems to completely transform every molecule of this body, changes the physical substance of this form I inhabit. Such has been the result of association with this beloved guide. Yet when he leaves, and I would return to my day-to-day activities, I have found that my mind becomes less subtle. The cells of my body seem to become more material, denser, rather than made of light and sentience.

What this internal guru has done for me and what I have been privileged to witness him do for others continues to astound me. It isn't easy to put it into words. I have often felt that I have been given a gift not only for me but for others as well, a gift that has allowed me to have an intimate firsthand experience of the omnipresent, compassionate manifestation of the Satguru.

The Self as One

Although in the silence of the depths of meditation, I feel that unitary consciousness, a more profound experience at this present stage, has been realizing that with eyes open or with eyes closed, the Self is ever one. Whether in samadhi, absorbed awareness, or fully alert in this world of forms, the Self is one. To me now, knowing the Self is knowing the One in everything, in pleasure and in pain, in happiness and in sorrow, in passion and in detachment, in bliss and in the world.

The wisdom I seek to integrate deeply and fully into my being stems from the teachings I am being given and the direct experience I am being shown. I have continued my meditations, but no longer, as when I was younger, do my deepest experiences tend to come in the silence of my reflection. Often, the most enlightening experiences tend to be associated with the manifestation of Baba's intuitional flow, the descending energies of divine waves of bliss, and the subtle perceptual field it creates.

At times my Baba is completely incomprehensible to me. What I see occurring defies my understanding of reality. It defies my knowledge of the known universe. It defies everything I have been taught, or understood in my upbringing, in this society. It goes into the realm of the mystical. It is a force of great compassion, which brings wisdom, love, and deep healing to living beings and shows them divinity. This force, this presence, is not a physical person. This body is the physical person. Yet it is not the source of this vast presence.

This Presence has a subtle intuitional relationship with each and every one of us; is in a cosmic dance with every living being. It is as if this body, being in a place, speaking the words coming forward from this wave of grace, is only an anchor to a particular point in time and space. Words are being spoken, but something else is happening, something much deeper, subtle, and profound. For those whose minds are quiet, who have a true love for divinity and are moving in a wave with Baba, this flow gives something—and I am astounded. I am humbled and awed to perceive the greatness of Divinity and the profound ways presence interfaces with people.

The full manifestation of this wave of Guru has gradually increased, just as Baba said it would back in 1990. Slowly over the years, this flow of guidance has grown and evolved, becoming more manifest. It has grown to a deeper state of bhava, immersion, in which Baba's presence has become closer to me. As time passes, I find I am melded more deeply into my Beloved. At times, I feel as if I cease to be a separate being, falling back, dissolving into Baba—for a time, only the Beloved abides.

Chapter XIII
The Teacher and Teachings

I feel as if I stand in two worlds: half of me in my body, in my persona, in my humanness, and the other half with my Beloved. I stand in two worlds.

When the weight shifts to the foot with my humanness, I'm a very ordinary person with ordinary needs and feelings, ordinary joys and enjoyments, natural human struggles and issues, happy feelings, sad feelings, fears, anger, and the gamut of human experience.

Then a time comes when my weight shifts, moving from one foot to the other. I feel the presence of the Beloved, a deep light, an unconditional love, a presence in which all knowledge exists. As this deepens within me, it begins to permeate my entire being.

My mind becomes filled with white light. This body becomes suffused with presence, as if every cell is permeated by it. And there is a deep, deep compassion that fills me. I become that love, that compassion. The presence of the Beloved engulfs this body and this mind and is all that exists.

As the weight shifts yet deeper onto this foot, into this reality, the separation of Guru and self dissolves. This body, this mind becomes permeated by presence, by the Beloved. To one degree or another, for some few minutes, an hour, a few hours, a day, a few days, a few weeks—to one degree or another, this immersion abides.

Then the weight shifts again to the human foot that rests in the human world, in a very ordinary person, with ordinary fears, sorrows and disappointments, ordinary needs, attachments, and losses. I begin to feel I am only this person—this very worldly human being—but just next to me, just behind me, behind the facade of me, is my Beloved, always there, always with me.

Then again, it is shifting, the Beloved comes close, comes near, and I begin to melt into him—white light dissolving my mind. Presence comes; all knowledge is in the divine guide, past, present, and future; the whole universe, planets, stars, galaxies, everything, all within the Beloved.

The Beloved takes form as my Baba; the Beloved becomes pure light, deep and endless compassion—and the words flow through this body like drops of nectar, teardrops of the Beloved, given into the world of form. This body is permeated; the Beloved alone exists; myself, my Beloved, we are one.

Again, my weight shifts towards the other foot that rests in the human world, and I am living an ordinary life with issues and struggles and enjoying everyday things: family, friends, a good movie, a good book. A very ordinary person living an ordinary life.

I do not own the Beloved. I cannot call the Beloved. The Beloved is—always there. The Beloved comes and permeates this existence. This Beloved is not an empty nothing. This Beloved is not simply a peaceful feeling. This Beloved is so much more than simple awareness.

My Beloved is like a thousand suns, a light so bright it stuns the mind. My Beloved is compassion so great there is nothing else. My Beloved is a love so strong that all human love is simply a dim reflection. My Beloved is the source, the home, beyond words to describe, the very source of every living being, the home that all long to find, the one true Self of all beings.

My Beloved is my Guru Deva, my Satguru, my closest companion, my own Self, not the self of the body-mind but the Self of the self. My Beloved is a love so great that in its presence, all cry. None can hold their form. None can bear the sweetness of that love.

My Beloved is the truth of all that is, is the love that cannot die, is the light that shines and stuns and dissolves all into itself. It is not a passive existence. It is a love that cares more than can be imagined, a love so deep that all love is its reflection. A truth so real all else is an illusion.

To be in the presence of the Beloved is to dissolve all dualities. Who can stand? Who can exist in this presence? It is impossible.

And then my Beloved steps back a little, and I am an ordinary human being in an ordinary life. But I know, even in my everyday human life, that I have met the Beloved and that one is more beautiful than can be known, more profound than the human mind can comprehend.

I know,
For I have met the Beloved.

The Awakening

In the early years of Baba's presence, the contrast bothered me when I saw these two sides of my existence. How could it be that when my inner guru was near, all seemed to flow naturally into unity, and when I was away from his presence, my reality could become so mundane? As the experience of transition from immersion in the divine Beloved to daily life inevitably occurred again and again for me over the years, I had trouble grasping the association of these two very different realities.

It was not that my day-to-day family life was unpleasant. I dearly loved my family and enjoyed the activities of my life. Yet my daily life was in complete contrast and juxtaposition to the intense spiritual energies that manifested during training programs and retreats. During these worldly times when Baba's flow was not manifesting, I would feel disconnected from myself—disassociated—as if I had merged into the world again but somehow could not find myself there.

This dichotomy seemed unnatural, and over time, a strong need arose in me to somehow integrate these two aspects and make my inner and outer lives one. I needed to find the intersection between my two worlds. The search to authentically understand and integrate the two sides of my life experience led me deeper into the realms of the unconditioned and the nondual.

As I reflect, this separation between spiritual states of being and worldly life has been my struggle from the beginning. Along with doubt and difficulty trusting, rejection of the world I saw as mundane and superficial plagued my spirit and obstructed my path. Yet through my exposure to spiritual love, the unitary whole of Being grew, along with the perception of all existence as the body of the infinite Beloved. I discovered the One Beloved embodied in the play of creation, appearing to be many but remaining ever One. As this perception grew, so did the ecstatic experience of unitary Oneness, both in this world and in the bliss realms, the Beloved of my heart abiding everywhere.

As awareness of this grew and the ecstatic love spilled over, the mind more easily gave way to the Beloved, and though I lived in the world, transparency began to form even in mundane life. I began to realize all is indeed Brahma; all is the Beloved. The world is not ordinary but a vibrant expression of the Infinite One.

The Infinite is Within Us and All Around Us

I began to see my beautiful guide within, my Baba—who is bringing me from darkness to light—as the manifestation of that which has always been and always will be, the one Self, the one unconditional love, taking form in the dance of creation.

As this knowing has grown, so has the perception that enjoying a good movie or a book, going for a walk with a friend, or even getting upset about something, or worried, or even being sad, is all the play of eternal Being manifesting in the dance of life. I began to perceive that all that surrounds me, all that I experience is my Beloved. There is no place, no time that One is not present. Timeless, eternal love, that One dances in all experiences, even when painful. Life and death come and go. Health and illness, pleasure and pain, youth and old age—all play out in the body of the Beloved of the heart. In a love so precious, so eternal, that there are no words to describe it, this dance of life plays out.

Deeply knowing this, the joy of being has grown; acceptance of what is has become more prominent. It does not mean I do not lose touch at times or that I do not suffer. Yet I have come to understand all of life's challenges, even forgetting, as the dance with the Beloved. When I forget, then, again, the joy of remembering returns, and I see my Beloved all around me—in the animals, in the trees, in a blade of grass. Even my body, breath, and thoughts are his form. Until the ordinary world transmutes—and setting aside my perceptions of form, setting aside my idea of me, I fall back into the One.

The Teacher

I understand my internal guru, Baba, to be a manifestation of the subtle vibrations of the Infinite One. Embodying for me as Shabda Brahma, or subtle sound, he manifests inner guidance. My physical guru, Anandamurti Baba, is said to be an embodiment of Taraka Brahma, the tangential point between the manifest and the unmanifest universe. Encompassing all that is, this limitless essence is the real Guru. Indeed, it is my experience that there is no limit to the true nature of Guru. A guru in form is a doorway through which this infinite One may be known.

My physical guru, Shrii Shrii Anandamurti, would say that Shiva, or pure consciousness, and Shakti, the creativity of nature, together compose Brahma. Brahma pervades the formless and formed universe. Omniscient, beyond description, the very fabric of all that is, Brahma or God is the Ultimate Reality, the true guru.

Whether the experience of a guru is internal, as it is for me with my Baba, or is with an external person, the true guru is a manifestation of Ultimate Reality. The physical guru is a man or a woman, like any of us. They have a body and body-related mind with cultural and other learned limitations. But the Divine One who can flow into and through a human being is the one who is Guru.

I have experienced my Baba in Shrii Shrii Anandamurti, my physical guru, but I have never thought of him as centered in the person who lived in India. To me, the guru is not a person but the infinite Brahma, the One Nondual Divine Existence. Yet that immortal Self of our self can manifest through subtle waves and within a living being.

My physical guru, who lived in India, was a vehicle for something great, something beyond human.

People say that as a child, Baba was called Prabhat until one day, as a boy of about five, he was wandering in the woods and encountered a column of light. The boy asked the column's name, and it told him it was Shrii Shrii Anandamurti. The light then moved forward and merged with the boy, who then took the name Shrii Shrii Anandamurti. Like this, the mystic stories go on, and great spiritual teachers come to the earth, not by learning and intellect, but by the grace of God. The Sublime embraces them, and the Infinite finds a way to speak to us in a form we can comprehend. The man in India and my Baba have both been forms through which that one true Guru, the Infinite One, has embodied for me in the dance of love and Self-discovery.

This same truth I have realized in my personal experience is recognized in traditional Indian texts. The *Guru Gita*, an ancient Indian text that describes the nature of the true Guru, gives great insight into the true Guru in the following stanzas. They are often chanted together as a puja, or offering, to the true Guru.

Akhanda mandala karam, Vyaptam yena cara caram
Tat padam darshitam yena, Tasmae shrii Guruave namah.
To the One revealed in the eternal mandala of creation
Who permeates both the moving and the unmoving,
To that esteemed Guru, I pay my salutations.

Ajinana timir andhasya, Jinanainjana shala kaya
Caksurun militam yena, Tasmae shrii Guruave namah.
To that divine Being, who, by applying the ointment of knowl-
edge, opens the eyes of one blinded by the darkness of igno-
rance. To that respected Guru, I pay my salutations.

Gurur Brahma Gurur Vishnu, Guru Devo Maheshvarah
Gurureva Parama Brahma, Tasmae shrii gurauve namah.
The Guru is Brahma, the Creator,
The Guru is Vishnu, the preserver,
The Guru is Shiva, the Destroyer of Ignorance,
The Guru is none other than the Infinite One, Parama Brahma
To that divine Guru, I surrender.

This ancient prayer describes the true nature of the Guru/God/Self. Over time, I have come to feel that the Satguru, the true Guru, is an eternal, non-corporeal existence that can manifest through human forms but is always infinite, pure, omnipresent, without divisions, and ever unbound.

That essence may manifest in different forms but is ever self-resplendent. The Guru takes form to guide and love, to draw living beings home to the One. Guru may manifest as an animal spirit, a sunrise, a bird chirping, or a babbling brook. The Infinite speaks with many voices for those with eyes to see and ears to hear. A deeply immersed person may embody the Guru, but the Guru is never the form. As the ancient texts espouse, the Guru is the Infinite One, *Parama Brahma.* Many are the forms through which the Guru can be known, yet the Guru remains one. Again, the yogis say Guru, God, and Self are One. There is only one Guru, one God, one Self of all beings.

Guru is not simply a man or a woman, not even a god or goddess, though the Guru may be seen in these. The Guru is that aspect of the cosmic existence that guides living beings from darkness to light, from death to immortality. The Guru embodies in unbound compassion, endless grace, unconditioned love, true wisdom, and the exquisite beauty of being. A guide to those seeking the depths, the Guru may come as a man or woman to teach and assist on the path or appear to you in subtle form to dance with you in love. The Guru has a personal relationship with every living being, as well as being the One who flung the stars into the firmament.

The Teachings

In my personal experience, the Guru has appeared in subtle form as Baba and has given teachings that help explain a deeper understanding. When that one softly speaks to me or through me to others, it says clearly what I, as my small ego self, cannot begin to write about the truth of Being.

The infinite Brahma is everywhere, amid everything. There is no one, nothing, outside of this divinity. It remains within you and around you.

The illusion of a separate "I," the illusion of being something apart from the Infinite One, is created when consciousness identifies with form. Within this, a belief forms in the mental construct of individuality, of separate existence. When in reality, all that you are, not only your spirit, your soul, but your mind, your thoughts, your experiences through the senses, your daily life, is the expression of the infinite Brahma. There is no one, nothing, apart from this.

Your happiness, sorrow, fear, and joy are all experiences of the infinite Brahma. For that which you are is part of an integrated, interwoven whole. That which you are is not separate from the whole—the idea of separateness is a belief created by embodiment. The Infinite One is closer than close because it is yourself, the Self of yourself.

That which you believe to be individuality is nothing but the expression of this Infinite One. You are the manifestation of the Infinite. That divine, eternal one without a second has no separateness. It is you. It is the ones you love. It is even the ones you despise. It is the light, and it is the darkness. It is love, and it is the capacity of hate. It is joy, and it is fear.

In the spectrum of creation, within the mind of the cosmic being, light, and shadow play, duality plays on and on, pleasure and pain, light and dark. All a part of that one cosmic play of being. And that which you call you, which expresses, feels, is the Infinite experiencing embodiment, experiencing the joy and the sorrow of this world. Having no separate existence, you are always whole.

That which you feel in the depth of your meditation, that which you feel in your devotion to God or Guru, in the deepest love of your heart, that is the truth, the light which shines, the light of your soul, the light of the love that is the Truth, that expresses in all creation.

You drift through the dream of this world. You think of yourself as small, limited. You want to escape pain and sorrow, grief and loss. You want to acquire love and happiness. You want to be loved by others. Such is the play of the belief in separation and the struggle to find wholeness. There is a bond between the dream and the dreamer, between the play and the puppeteer, for the play occurs in the imagination of the puppeteer. The dream is in the mind of the dreamer.

Just allow yourself to melt back, fall back, into the eternal. This is the true Yoga. And out of that comes the true knowledge, for all knowledge lies within you. But ultimately, there is no inner and outer. There is the shell of form, and the individual's mind is part of that shell. Because awareness, being, is embodied in the shell of the body, it assumes that there is something outside and something inside. But there is no truth to that. There is only infinite Being.

When the eyes are open and the mind awake, when the love of the Infinite showers across your being and you are immersed in that, the bird's song sings to you from the very depths of the soul of being. Those you love are the embodiments of the Infinite. All nature is the emanation of that One. For that One has embodied in all that is; there is no separation. The form is the illusion. Love divine is the medium of being. It is the presence of Truth.

When the dream covers the mind, you believe yourself to be the character in the dream. And you dance the dance, experience the highs and the lows. It is the joy of the Infinite to know duality. But then you return. Deep in your being, you return to that which you have always known, that which is core to you, that which is the Self of yourself. This God, this Guru of your heart, is always present.

The Guru says: "Where can I go? I am always here." There is no place to go. The One is everywhere. And when the noise in the mind settles in the depths of being, in the love, in the soul, there is a timelessness, a moment that has always been and always will be. For time does not move in the depths of your being. It is always now. It is always Truth.

Remember and practice until, where there has been the identity of you, as the form, as the dream, there, in that shell, is the one infinite Self, the one infinite Consciousness. There you abide—and not only in the body but in all that surrounds you. That which you have thought to be ordinary, when the eyes are open, is extraordinary. The elixir of life is all around you.

You know, people begin the path of meditation and Yoga by desiring this and desiring that. "I want to improve my health." "I want to become a great Yogi and have powers." "I want to be able to be unique and special." Hmm? Perhaps some thoughts like these have crossed your mind?

But as the mind grows in magnitude, as the true experiences of the Self emerge and dissolve the ego self, you unlock the assumptions and beliefs in the mind that have bound you. Then by the grace of that Infinite One, the shadows of illusion that have constricted you fade away, and knowledge of the truth comes. The motivation of Sadhana, meditation, changes entirely.

Once you have met the true Master, Beloved, there is no turning back. The heart is given, and the bond is established. Letting go of pride—pride in your humility, pride in your achievements, pride in your identity with your form, letting go, surrendering everything to the one great love—you are no longer separate.

When consciousness abides in form, it sees through eyes, hears through ears, and the dance of creation goes on being experienced. But you can rest in the knowledge that though you are in form, this experience of duality is not binding. Let go into the nonduality of being. Let that be all that is. Let go of your pride. Let go of your false humility that says, "Oh no, this is too much for me." This is a barrier, an obstacle in the mind. "I'm not worthy." This also is an obstacle in the mind. You are the child of the great. Be innocent. Be open. Let that one bring you home. This is the Sadhana once other barriers have fallen. Be truly humble and accept that the Beloved of your heart is all that is. There is no separate self, only a dream.

And there is nothing wrong with the dream. Just know that it's a dream. All lies in the Beloved. Those you love are the Beloved in form. Where can they go to be separate from you? Nowhere, nowhere. This is the Sadhana, the love that never dies, the Guru that always is.

These teachings that flow through point to the unitary whole of being. The bliss that often accompanies them in the talks has aligned my heart. When these teachings flow from the Guru, they often become the reality that seems so natural, so obvious.

Yet it takes intention to stay with the nondual perception of wholeness. Once the Presence is not in focus, it is so easy to slip again into "you and me," "I and mine," apart from you. It is easy to forget that we are all one and that divine love is a vibrant essence that permeates all life. It takes intention to stay in remembrance. When I sit at my desk, it takes awareness to really see the plant before me, to experience the living and breathing being filled with life force, a vibrant creation that embodies the Infinite in plant form.

When I embrace this experience, the mundane and ordinary become extraordinary. When I embrace this knowledge, all the ups and downs of my life seem a little less important, and the vibrant beauty of every person I meet, and the animals and plants, astounds me. I look out across the mountains and feel honored to see the beauty of this world, alive and vital, the Divine in form. When the Beloved is all around, in form, where is there to run to? What is there to run from? The yogis say that eyes open or eyes closed, it is the same. The Infinite is everywhere.

When I reflect upon my journey of the soul, I see that so much of the turbulence and suffering I experienced was due to my not fully understanding what was happening to me, combined with my inability to trust. Doubt and lack of faith in my inner guide made it a harder journey than it needed to be, though I do not think this journey is easy for anyone who sincerely seeks to know the Divine.

It is not a journey for the faint of heart. It inevitably involves facing your inner demons and coming face to face with your deepest fears, walking through the darkness to the light. It is not for those who do not want to look behind the curtain. Those who can content themselves with the surface enjoyments of life and have not the need to search for deeper meaning and truth will not brave this journey to the core of their being.

But for one whose spirit is restless and who yearns to find their deepest truth, the rewards of this journey are untold. It is impossible to put into words the beauty of the soul and the indescribable, unnamable essence in the core of being. The mystics of the ages, from all across the world and from all cultures, have been touched by something so profound and great that it cannot be named. The truth of it, the beauty, are beyond words. Only its footprints can be seen, manifest in love, truth, and bliss beyond understanding.

Connection to Source

Some further relevant teachings were given recently to a small gathering.

More Teachings

Beyond time and space, beyond past, present, and future, lies an eternal unity. The vastness of untold universes, with billions of stars shedding planets with untold life, is all a part of an infinite, interwoven, interconnected web of existence. This vast web of creativity and creation exists within the consciousness of being—beyond time, beyond space, beyond duality.

The essence of being, in which the physical universe arises, is the ever-present, omniscient, unitary whole some refer to as Parama Purusha or God. All creation abides within this substantive existence, within the consciousness and the mind of the infinite Being. From this consciousness, blended with the motion of creativity in Mother Nature and her five elements, the manifestation of all life unfolds.

Like a grain of sand on a vast beach, you abide within this whole. You are part of this vastness, part of this interwoven, interconnected web of life. You are consciousness embodied in form within the web of life, within the awareness and intelligence of the universal whole. When the dream of time, space, and movement falls away, when the dream of "I" and "mine" is shed, what remains here, now?

Within the puddle, the moon shines bright. Within the sea, the drop of water is held and dissolves. Where is the difference between you and that most Beloved of your heart? That one does not stand outside of you in some far distant place or some high holy heaven you must strive to achieve. That one is the Self of yourself, always with you, closer than close. In its wave of infinite love, there is no division between "I" and "thou."

Who are you to believe yourself to be separate? You attribute good and bad; you attribute right and wrong; you attribute gain and loss. You take on these attributions, and you identify with the experiences. But to whom do those experiences belong?

Child, look into your heart, deep, beyond all the identities with experiences. Let them go. Let them go. You are a grain of sand, the dust on the wind—yet within you abides the light of the Infinite, the love of the Supreme. You, the dust in the wind of this infinite Existence, are composed of none other than that divine Self, that divine Being.

You are in the vast, interwoven network of life. You are in the smallest molecule, in the waves and particles. You are in the firmament and the vastness of the universe. You fly on the wings of an eagle, soar to the depths of the sea in the whale, live in the breeze, in the wind, in the earth, in the stars; in all creation, you are. A drop of water and the whole, you are.

Yoga is the science of unfolding this truth within you, erasing the misconceptions of the mind, erasing false identities, and coming to know your true nature. Tantra is the science of this transmutation. There is one Guru, one God, one Self, one Truth. The bliss of knowing, the light of love—this is your nature. Awaken from the dream. Arise.

It has taken me many years to really understand the teachings and to learn to see the Divine. Perhaps I am a bit hardheaded, but I couldn't get it. I wanted to run away from pain and heartache. I tried to avoid the pain of loss and separation, but the path lies not in running from this world but in expanding the experience of divinity to include the world. This has required a radical adjustment of my thinking, which has taken time. Such is my guide's infinite patience and grace that he has stayed with me through the thick and thin of this journey.

My childhood vision of a pyramid or triangle leading to a point where I would know my destiny proved to be real. I found my destiny, the work I came here to do. I found my commitment to Guru and guide, a commitment from a time before I can remember—and, in the process, I discovered the sublime. I have found there is only the One, dancing in all of the forms and colors of creation, including this which I have called mine—and that which you have called yours.

Deepening

The moon is clear,
Silver rays kiss the earth,
The night air is warm,
And clouds fill the sky.
Wisps frosted with moonlight.

I look up at the moon,
And you are there.
In moon, moonlight, and in shadows
All around me, you have embodied,
In this night of creation

Bathing me in your silver rays
You embrace me with your night,
Caressing me tenderly with night breezes
Kissing my hair with moonlight

Melting in you, I dance with arms raised,
Heart awash in love and grace
A tender moment cast forth by you,
Played in the halls of eternity.

The years have moved past as the sun turns night into day, and the moon calls forth the evening stars. As the circles around the sun have come and gone, the dance with the Infinite has played out, and I have settled into the peace of being. Dancing with the Beloved, I have looked into that one's eyes and become speechless in awe. I have surrendered definitions of self to the one who has flung the stars into the heavens and captured my heart in unconditioned love.

My time spent now in ordinary tasks: writing, reading, being with friends, being with my husband and grown sons, and assisting others on their journeys, is not apart from my Beloved. My life is ordinary, except nothing is ordinary when I notice the Beloved in all the manifest glory of form and change while ever remaining changeless. The grace of this presence has become like an old friend, always there, always accessible. The process of connection slowly deepened over time, and the separation diminished.

I have felt the grace that brings my two worlds together. At times melted into my Beloved's flow, I ceased to experience the separation between myself and my Baba. My small self, dissolving into the flow of grace, ceases to be. Where only a moment ago there was a personality with varying experiences and opinions, now no one is there, nothing present but the immortal, immanent vastness of Being, forming words, bringing light to the earth plane. At those moments, I cease to be as I have known myself. Absorbed, melted back into the Beloved, divinity alone abides.

Then again, the moment is over, and duality steps between. But forever, I know, deep within, beyond the scope of persona, we are ever united. The mind dances in the world of forms, experiencing the residuals of attachments and desires playing out. And then again, I turn, and the Beloved is there. My being melts for a moment into that One. There are no words, only the power of love, the soft embrace of pure being in which I and thou disappear for a moment, for minutes, an hour, or perhaps eternity.

Glossary of Sanskrit & Other Relevant Terms

Acharya – Teacher or instructor of meditation and in spiritual matters. One who teaches by their exemplary conduct.

Ajna Chakra – The third eye. The chakra located one finger's width above the eyebrows in the center of the head.

Anahata Chakra – The heart chakra. Located between the breasts.

Anandamurti Arati – Traditional ceremony showing respect for a god, guru, or deity that usually involves circling a flame before the person or god's image while chanting holy names. In this case, a ritual honoring the guru Shrii Shrii Anandamurti.

Asanas – Physical postures in yoga

Ashram – Spiritual hermitage or center for spiritual living and teachings.

Ashtanga Yoga – The union of the eight limbs of yoga into one complete, holistic system. First codified by Patanjali in the Yoga Sutras, the eight limbs include the yamas (abstinences), niyamas (observances), asanas (postures), pranayama (breathing), pratyahara (withdrawal), dharana (concentration), dhyana (meditation) and samadhi (absorption).

Baba – Father or affectionate term for an elder; often used for spiritual masters. Also, in its most esoteric form, it can mean Divine Beloved.

Baba Nam Kevalam – Mantra meaning "Love is all there is."

Bhakti – Devotion or love towards a deity, guru, or god.

Bhava – Feeling. A subtle mood of spiritual absorption.

Bodhi – Enlightenment. Awakening. The Bodhi Tree is where Buddha became enlightened.

Brahma (or Brahman) – Denotes God. The name of the manifest and unmanifest universe as a whole. With a long "a" at the end, it indicates the creator god in Hinduism, Brahmā.

Dadajii – Affectionate term for an elder brother. Monks were called Dadajii in Anandamurti Baba's tradition.

Dharma – Duty, righteousness, or cosmic order moving towards the Infinite. Collective or personal calling or purpose in life.

Dharmachakra – The wheel of Dharma. Also, the name of the group meditations in my tradition.

Dhoti – Traditional men's garment that is a loose, cloth pant.

Didi – Older sister. Nuns are often referred to as Didi.

Fatwa – Legal opinion in Islamic law.

Gita – Refers to the Bhagavad Gita, a 700-verse Hindu scripture.

Goonda – Thug, bully, or cutthroat.

Gopi – Female cowherd and devotee of Krishna.

Gurkha knife – A traditional long knife with a curved blade.

Guru – Teacher or spiritual guide. In Sanskrit, Gu means ignorance, and ru indicates the remover (of darkness or ignorance). Thus, the Guru is the remover of illusion or ignorance.

Guru Deva – Divine teacher.

Guru Gita – Song of the Guru. A traditional text that describes the Guru.

Guru Shakti – Power or grace of the Guru. The power of God's grace.

Ista Deva – The chosen deity or guru that a person is devoted to.

Jagreti – An ashram or center for spiritual living and teachings. It also means "awakening" or "consciousness" in Sanskrit/Hindi.

Karmapa – Title for the head of one school of Tibetan Buddhism.

Kirtan – Devotional song or chant containing sacred names. Also, a dance done while chanting the names of God in the Bhakti Yoga tradition, first initiated by Chaitanya Prabhu. Chanting *Baba Nama Kevalam* and dancing kirtan was part of Shrii Shrii Anandamurti's spiritual practices.

Kosha – Layer or sheath of the mind, often referring to layers of the self.

Krishna – An avatar of Lord Vishnu and a central figure in the Mahabharata.

Kula Guru – Family or ancestral teacher. The guide of the kula kundalini.

Kula Kundalini – Primordial energy that lies at the base of the spine and rises with spiritual unfoldment into higher states.

Kundalini – Spiritual energy believed to lie dormant at the base of the spine that, when it rises to the top of the head, brings enlightenment.

Kurta – Loose, collarless shirt worn in many regions of South Asia.

Lungi – Traditional Indian garment worn around the waist in place of pants.

Ma – Mother

Mahat – Cosmic intelligence or great principle. The "I exist" sentiment.

Mantra – Sacred name, word, or phrase used in meditation.

Mudra – Symbolic hand gesture.

Muladhara Chakra – Base chakra located at the base of the spine.

Nadii – Channels through which prana flows in the body. Kundalini and spiritual awakening involve the Sushumna, Ida, and Pingala channels or Nadiis.

Namaskar – Greeting or salutation meaning "I bow to the Divinity within you."

Nyingma – Oldest school of Tibetan Buddhism.

Om – Om or aum (pronounced ah-uu-mm) is a sacred sound considered by many ancient philosophical texts to be the sound of the universe, encompassing all other sounds within it. It is defined by Hindu and Yogic scripture as being the primordial sound of creation and the original vibration of the universe.

Parama Brahma – Ultimate or supreme reality.

Parama Purusha – Supreme being or consciousness.

Parvati – Consort of Shiva.

Prana – Life force or vital energy. It flows through the Nadiis or energy channels in the body.

Pranam – A gesture of respect or salutation often made toward a deity, guru, or revered person.

Pranayama – Breath control practices in yoga.

Puja – A ritual of offerings and respect to the Guru or God.

Radha – Consort of Krishna.

Rama – Avatar of Vishnu and protagonist of the Ramayana.

Sadhana – Spiritual practice.

Sahasvara Chakra – Crown chakra located at the top of the head.

Samadhi – State of intense concentration or union with the divine.

Samskaras – Mental impressions or imprints within the mind. They become Karma when expressed.

Sangha – Spiritual community.

Sannyasin – Renunciant or ascetic.

Sari – Traditional Indian female garment.

Satguru – True guru.

Sattvic – Pure, true; one of the three gunas or fundamental building block qualities of creation in Indian thought. Sattva—Sentient, Rajas—mutative, Tamas—Static.

Shabda Brahma – God as sound or word. Also called Shabda Brahman.

Shaktipat – A transfer of energy from a guru to a disciple.

Shiva – One of the principal Hindu deities, known as the destroyer of ignorance. He is believed by many to be a historical figure and the father of Tantra, living some 7,000 to 10,000 years ago. Shiva is also used as a synonym for infinite consciousness.

Sita – Consort of Rama.

Sufi – Islamic mystic

Swami – Hindu or Yogic monk. One who is the master/owner of oneself, a member of a swami order.

Tandava – The dance of Shiva.

Tantra – Practices and rituals to worship the divine. A spiritual path leading from darkness to light. A set of practices to bring people in contact with the divine energy within their bodies (Kundalini Shakti) via movement, chanting, breathing, and meditation.

Taraka Brahma – The liberator aspect of Brahma. The tangential point between the manifest and unmanifest universe. Shrii Shrii Anandamurti was said to be a manifestation of Taraka Brahma.

Thangka – Tibetan Buddhist painting on cotton or silk.

Thik hai – Hindi word for ok or yes. Often said twice with sideways head nods.

Tulku – Incarnate lama in Tibetan Buddhism.

Vedic – Pertaining to the Vedas, ancient Indian scriptures.

Yoga – To yoke together. To unite the small self with the larger self. Yoga includes physical, mental, and spiritual practices. It first originated in ancient India and was codified by the sage Patanjali in his Yoga Sutras.

Yoga Maya – Divine illusion. Often refers to the aspect of Maya that leads beings back towards the One.

Yoga Sutras – Foundational text on yoga by Patanjali.

Note: Some words, like "Goonda," "Gurkha," and "Thangka," are not Sanskrit but have been included for clarity. The list represents a mix of Sanskrit, Hindi, Tibetan, Nepali, and other regional terms.

About the Author

$\mathcal{D}$r. Maetreyii Ma Nolan is a distinguished author, licensed Clinical Psychologist, and president of Ananda Guru Kula, a non-profit organization devoted to spreading yoga's wisdom teachings. With roles as the past founder and president of Ananda Seva Mission, a founding board member of the Kundalini Research Network, and a previous director of the Spiritual Emergency Network, she has long been a guiding light in the spiritual community.

Dr. Nolan is a psychologist in private practice, an Acharya or ordained Yogic Minister, a certified Yoga Therapist, and a 500-hour certified Yoga Teacher who combines clinical psychology with timeless insights from yogic teachings.

As a spiritual mentor, Maetreyii Ma provides Baba Talks, teaches classes, and guides students in her mentoring program. She hosts webinars, retreats, and seminars, creating spaces where individuals can explore and experience the Divine.

A mother of two grown sons, she lives with her husband in their ashram community in Northern California's San Francisco Bay Area, where she continues to write, teach, and inspire – extending an open invitation to all to explore the transformative power of connecting with the Divine.

Learn More about Maetreyii Ma and her Teachings!

Visit Ma's website, learn about her books, and explore the teachings & opportunities offered!

www.yogaMa.info

Stay in touch with Ma and her upcoming offerings!
Stay Connected and Join our Mailing List!
Also, get a free mini book on Mysticism at
www.yogama.info

Follow us on Social Media
www.maetreyiima.org
https://linktr.ee/maetreyiima
Listen and follow Maetreyii Ma's Podcast
https://www.babatalks.info

Or go to Ma's YouTube Channel to watch some intuitive Baba talks at
https://www.youtube.com/@maetreyiima7

Other Publications by Maetreyii Ma

Books & Mini Books
Available Online or at Your Local Bookstore

Living Love The Yoga of Yama & Niyama

Dharma For Awakening and Social Change

Feminine Mysticism Secrets of the Empowered
Feminine

The Future is Bright Visions of the Future

Yoga Psychology Understanding & Awakening
Kundalini

For Bulk Ordering or More Information Contact
Ananda Guru Kula Publications
Santa Rosa, CA
anandagurukula@gmail.com
707-575-0886
www.MaetreyiiMa.org

*If this book speaks to you, please write a review and share
with others what this book has given to you*

OM SHANTI, SHANTI, SHANTI

Made in the USA
Middletown, DE
18 November 2023

42891780R00182